Ending the Civil War and Consequences for Congress

Perspectives on the History of Congress, 1801–1877

Donald R. Kennon, Series Editor

Congress and the Emergence of Sectionalism:
From the Missouri Compromise to the Age of Jackson,
edited by Paul Finkelman and Donald R. Kennon

In the Shadow of Freedom: The Politics of Slavery in the National Capital,
edited by Paul Finkelman and Donald R. Kennon

Congress and the Crisis of the 1850s, edited by Paul Finkelman
and Donald R. Kennon

Lincoln, Congress, and Emancipation, edited by Paul Finkelman
and Donald R. Kennon

Congress and the People's Contest: The Conduct of the Civil War,
edited by Paul Finkelman and Donald R. Kennon

Civil War Congress and the Creation of Modern America:
A Revolution on the Home Front, edited by Paul Finkelman and
Donald R. Kennon

Ending the Civil War and Consequences for Congress,
edited by Paul Finkelman and Donald R. Kennon

Ending the Civil War and Consequences for Congress

Edited by Paul Finkelman and Donald R. Kennon

PUBLISHED FOR THE
UNITED STATES CAPITOL HISTORICAL SOCIETY
BY OHIO UNIVERSITY PRESS • ATHENS

Ohio University Press, Athens, Ohio 45701
ohioswallow.com
© 2019 by Ohio University Press
All rights reserved

To obtain permission to quote, reprint, or otherwise reproduce or distribute material from
Ohio University Press publications, please contact our rights and permissions department
at (740) 593-1154 or (740) 593-4536 (fax).

Printed in the United States of America
Ohio University Press books are printed on acid-free paper ∞™

29 28 27 26 25 24 23 22 21 20 19   5 4 3 2 1

Library of Congress Cataloging-in-Publication Data

. Names: Finkelman, Paul, 1949– editor. | Kennon, Donald R., 1948– editor.
Title: Ending the civil war and consequences for Congress / edited by Paul Finkelman
    and Donald R. Kennon.
Description: Athens : Published for the United States Capitol Historical Society by Ohio
    University Press, [2018] | Series: Perspective hist of congress 1801–1877 | Includes
    bibliographical references and index.
Identifiers: LCCN 2019004316| ISBN 9780821423370 (hardback) |
    ISBN 9780821446461 (pdf)
Subjects: LCSH: United States—History—Civil War, 1861–1865—Law and legislation. |
    Postwar reconstruction—Law and legislation—United States—History—19th century. |
    Civil rights—Law and legislation—United States—History—19th century. | United
    States. Congress—History—19th century. | United States—Politics and
    government—1865–1877. | BISAC: HISTORY / United States / Civil War
    Period (1850–1877). | LAW / Legal History.
Classification: LCC KF7221 .E53 2018 | DDC 349.7309/034—dc23
LC record available at https://lccn.loc.gov/2019004316

Contents

Paul Finkelman

Introduction   I

Carole Emberton

"A Hungry Belly and Freedom": Rations, Refugees,
and Reconstruction at the End of the Civil War   11

Lorien Foote

Federal Prisoners of War and the Long Recovery   24

Jenny Bourne

When Johnny Came Marching Home, What Did He Find?
A Look at the Postbellum U.S. Economy   39

Anne Sarah Rubin

An Infamous Disregard? Sherman's March and the Laws of War   54

Paul Finkelman

The Fourteenth Amendment and the Joint Committee
on Reconstruction   74

Peter Wallenstein

Historicizing the Politics of Reconstruction: Congress
and the Fourteenth Amendment, Section 2   103

William E. Nelson

Sectionalism, the Fourteenth Amendment, and the End
of Popular Constitutionalism   135

vi *Contents*

Clay Risen

The Civil War at 100, the Civil War at 150: Commemoration,
Identity, and the Changing Shape of National Memory   149

Contributors   157

Index   159

Paul Finkelman

Introduction

AFTER FOUR YEARS of intense and brutally bloody combat, the Civil War was finally over. The Southern experiment in treason had ended in total defeat. The Confederate capital, Richmond, was a burned-out hulk (figs. 1 and 2). Across the eleven states that had formed the Confederacy, railroads were in ruins, factories (and some cities) were in ashes, and many farms were unplowed and unplanted. As Anne Sarah Rubin notes in her essay on Sherman's army, in some parts of the South—Missouri, the Shenandoah Valley, and a sixty-mile-wide swath of Georgia and the Carolinas—homes, barns, and crops had been destroyed. In some places, civilians had been displaced by combat in their neighborhoods or by armies on both sides, who forced them out of harm's way, even when they wanted to remain in their homes.

Even in places untouched by combat or unvisited by armies from either side, the effects of the war were visible. Four million African Americans were no longer slaves. At least 100,000 former slaves returned to the South in U.S. Army uniforms, some still carrying their muskets and bayonets. These combat veterans were not only willing but also able to defend the freedom they had helped win for themselves and their families. But their numbers would ultimately be insufficient to preserve black equality in the face of Southern white terrorism and viciously creative Southern state legislatures and politicians. The Fourteenth Amendment, as chapters by Paul Finkelman, William E. Nelson, and Peter Wallenstein show, would be necessary to

I

FIG. 1. April 1865 photograph by Andrew J. Russell shows the destruction of the waterfront across the canal basin in Richmond with the Virginia State Capitol and the U.S. Custom House in the distance. *(Library of Congress Prints and Photographs Division)*

FIG. 2. Ruins on Carey Street in Richmond, photographed at the end of the war by Andrew J. Russell. *(Library of Congress Prints and Photographs Division)*

secure legal citizenship for former slaves, but as we know, enforcement would remain insufficient for a century.

On the other side of the equation, nearly 300,000 Southern white men would never return home—they lay buried all over the former Confederacy, as well as in other parts of the rest of the United States. Probably 200,000 or more Confederates came home visibly wounded, while countless others carried the mental scars of combat. Lorien Foote reminds us that more than 160,000 Confederate prisoners of war (POWs) returned as well, all carrying with them the scars and nightmares of war that would last forever. "Most former POWs," whether Confederate or U.S., "never fully recovered from their captivity." Even those who went on to have successful lives were plagued by "physical ailments" while "sharp, clear, unwanted memories of life in prison were deeply embedded in their minds."

Northern families, veterans, and returning POWs also suffered grievously from the war. The U.S. Army, despite its vast resources and logistical successes during the war, was unable to provide medical care, food, or even full transportation for POWs rescued from Confederate captivity at the end of the war. Most POWs got home soon after the war ended, although their journeys, as Foote teaches us, were sometimes harrowing and unnecessarily hard. The last U.S. POW to return home arrived in 1889. He suffered from amnesia for a quarter century before miraculously regaining his memory and his family.

Because most of the war was fought in the Confederacy, and the Confederacy suffered a much higher proportion of casualties (killed, wounded, and captured), the effects of the conflict were much greater and more obvious in the South. The social conditions of the South had been turned upside down, or at least fundamentally altered, and the economy was in tatters. Former slaves as well as the former master class suffered from physical deprivation and a lack of food. Ironically, as Carole Emberton demonstrates, these costs were disproportionately borne by former slaves, who had virtually no resources or land when the fighting ended. After the war, former slaves faced hunger and even starvation, but as Emberton points out, in the aftermath of the conflict "the majority of food relief went to white refugees."

The lack of food, housing, and other necessities in part stemmed from a final cruelty of slavery: whites who had lived for so long on the labor of slaves were unwilling to help feed the newly freed blacks, and in the immediate aftermath of the war many former slaves had virtually no access to land, seed, farm animals, and equipment to grow their own crops. The United States had spent fortunes on a war to end slavery but was structurally and ideologically ill equipped to provide for the basic needs of those who were now free.

In addition, of course, the war had destroyed much of the agricultural infrastructure necessary for basic food production. The destruction of Sherman's march through Georgia and the Carolinas illustrates this. Rubin correctly reminds us that Sherman's March to the Sea was hardly the barbaric assault on humanity that lost-cause partisans and novelists like Margaret Mitchell fantasize about. In reality, Sherman's march was nothing like the German invasion of Belgium in World War I, the German invasion of eastern and western Europe in World War II, or the Soviet counterattack in the same war. Sherman's soldiers took food and forage as needed for their army, and confiscated or destroyed matériel that was useful to the enemy; but soldiers were prohibited from wanton looting, and the army never countenanced murdering or raping civilians. Sherman approved the executions of his own troops convicted in court martials for such behavior. Sherman's march was not the horror show that some historians, novelists, or moviemakers portrayed it a half century ago. Still, it was an awful experience for civilians who lived through it, as well as for the Confederate soldiers who were battered and defeated in battle after battle for more than a year.

Nevertheless, as Clay Risen tells us, the memory filtered by a century and a half of myths and some history remains contested. Even if the Civil War is no longer the "felt" history it once was, Risen reminds us that it remains very much a contested history.

The costs of the war—human and financial—as well as the profound political and legal changes stemming from the war led to a massive readjustment in demography, social services, economics, politics, and law. The immediate costs in lives and blood were staggering. More than 2.6 million men served in the U.S. Army and Navy, and more than a million in the Confederate military.[1] This constituted more than 10 percent of the entire nation's population in 1860. About 360,000 U.S. soldiers and sailors died

---

[1]The website of the National Park Service lists 2,672,341 U.S. soldiers and estimates that the Confederate army had between 750,000 and 1.2 million soldiers. This site does not include naval service for either side or for irregulars and guerillas fighting for the Confederacy. National Park Service, "The Civil War," https://www.nps.gov/civilwar/facts.htm.

during the war, along with 290,000 Confederates. An additional 500,000 were wounded.[2] The number who returned with emotional scars and mental health issues is unknown. Because both sides were "Americans" before and after the war, these numbers are aggregated, at 650,000 "American" deaths in the war, although some scholars argue for a much larger figure.[3] This is more than all U.S. wartime fatalities in all other U.S. wars combined. In addition, unlike wars fought on foreign soil, some civilians died in the war and many others suffered grievously from the destruction of their homes and crops and the confiscation of food and farm animals. Northern civilians also suffered from the Confederate depredations, which were often far worse than those faced by Southerners. In Missouri, psychopathic Confederate killers "Bloody Bill" Anderson, Frank and Jesse James, and the Younger brothers murdered civilians and captured U.S. troops with a gory frenzy. Meanwhile, on the East Coast, Confederate soldiers under the command of Robert E. Lee kidnapped and enslaved free blacks living in the United States during Lee's Maryland campaign in 1862 and his Pennsylvania campaign in 1863, dragging them back to Virginia as his army retreated from its defeats at Antietam and Gettysburg. These acts violated all known and accepted rules of civilized warfare. Everywhere in the Western world it was considered a war crime to enslave civilians or to murder surrendering troops. But Confederates did both, with the tacit or active approval of their putative nation's high command and civilian leadership. Confederate troops in the South murdered and mutilated surrendering black troops at Fort Pillow and elsewhere; and as Foote notes in her chapter, at Dalton, Georgia, Confederates enslaved most of a regiment after it surrendered.

To understand the magnitude of the human cost of the war, it is useful to compare the Civil War casualties with the current U.S. population. In 2010 the United States had about ten times the population it had in 1860. Thus, a war of similar magnitude would lead to at least 6 million deaths and

---

[2] Claudia D. Goldin and Frank D. Lewis, "The Economic Cost of the American Civil War: Estimates and Implications," *Journal of Economic History* 35 (June 1975):299, 305.

[3] One such scholar claims that fatalities for both sides were between 650,000 and 850,000. Given this huge numerical spread, he settled on 750,000 as the right number. Guy Gugliotta, "New Estimate Raises Civil War Death Toll," *New York Times*, Apr. 2, 2012, https://www.nytimes.com/2012/04/03/science/civil-war-toll-up-by-20-percent-in-new-estimate.html. This higher number remains controversial, but if the higher figure turns out to be correct, it only underscores the huge human cost of the conflict.

4.75 million wounded soldiers. It is almost impossible to imagine a war of that magnitude in the modern era.

Because the war was fought on U.S. soil—or what would once again become U.S. soil after the defeat of the Confederacy—there were unprecedented social and economic costs to the conflict. The length of the war increased these costs. The war was more than twice as long as the two previous conflicts—the Mexican War and the War of 1812. This time line not only created greater suffering but led to increased destruction of nonmilitary property, especially in the Confederacy. Throughout the Confederacy, homes, factories, farms, and large parts of cities were destroyed. By 1865 many places in the South were devastated and in ruins. Before the people of the former Confederacy could fully feed themselves and regain economic stability and even prosperity, they had to rebuild much of what had been destroyed by the war. Thus, while peace meant an end to battles, it did not lead to an immediate end to human suffering.

Some of this destruction in the South resulted from the collateral damage of war or from battles actually being fought inside or around cities. Three separate battles were fought in and around the town of Fredericksburg, Virginia, and to this day the remains of dead soldiers are sometimes found. But some of this physical destruction was caused by retreating Confederate troops who burned their own warehouses and cities to prevent matériel from falling into the hands of their enemies. This scorched-earth policy in Georgia and the Carolinas did not do much to slow the advance of General Sherman's army, as it liberated hundreds of thousands of slaves in the Deep South while simultaneously destroying Confederate armies. But the policy did exacerbate poverty, hunger, and the lack of infrastructure and resources in the postwar South.

The financial cost of the war was truly profound. Careful economic historians conclude that the cost to the United States[4]—or the Union as it is often called—was about $4.5 billion, in 1860 dollars. Most of this went to paying and equipping soldiers. The estimate for the Confederate States of America was even larger, $5.8 billion, in 1860 dollars, even though the Confederacy had only about one-third as many people. Much of the cost to the

---

[4]"United States" refers to those states that remained loyal to the Constitution, and excludes the Confederate states, even though technically, at least as understood by the Lincoln administration, they were part of the United States.

Confederacy resulted from the loss of "physical capital," such as factories, railroads, buildings, and farm equipment.[5] The Confederate costs also include the loss of "economies of scale" due to the destruction of slavery.[6] These figures do not include the loss of capital owned by Southern whites due to the end of slavery. Ending slavery, after all, transferred value from masters to the former slaves, who now "owned" themselves. However, before and during the war, slaves were capital assets that could be sold, mortgaged, rented, and used as collateral for economic development. In addition, because of the continuing growth of the slave population, slaves represented an economic asset that was constantly increasing in value. Factoring in the loss of these assets increases the costs of the war to the white Confederates, who in fact seceded to protect and preserve slavery forever. The Emancipation Proclamation, the victory of the U.S. Army, and the Thirteenth Amendment not only transformed four million slaves into free people but also eliminated about $2 billion worth of capital in the former Confederacy.[7]

These costs can also be understood by per capita allocations. The United States (the Union) had three times the population of the Confederate states. Thus, the per capita cost of the war was $670 in the Confederacy but only $199 in the United States.[8] None of these figures include a value (how could we put a value on it?) for the emotional cost of more than 650,000 deaths and half a million wounded survivors.

The war left economic scars and trauma across the nation that mirrored the profound horrors of deaths and physical scars. Returning soldiers were traumatized in both sections, but much more in the South than in the North. U.S. soldiers returned victorious to a society that was hopeful of the future. Although as Foote notes, returning U.S. POWs suffered profoundly from the inability of the victorious nation to care for these men or even figure out how to help them get home. But when the veterans and former POWs

---

[5]Roger L. Ransom, "The Economics of the Civil War," http://eh.net/encyclopedia/the-economics-of-the-civil-war/. For somewhat different but similar calculations, see Goldin and Lewis, "The Economic Cost of the American Civil War," pp. 299, 305, 308, 321–22.

[6]Goldin and Lewis, "The Economic Cost of the American Civil War," p. 322.

[7]Ransom, "The Economics of the Civil War." This essay puts the cost of buying all the slaves in 1860 at $2.7 billion, but I have reduced that to account for the value of slaves in states that remained in the United States: Kentucky, Missouri, Maryland, Delaware, and what became West Virginia.

[8]Ransom, "The Economics of the Civil War."

did get home, they found that profound changes in Northern society made possible by the absence of slave owners in Congress promised a better future. The Homestead Act and the Transcontinental Railroad Act increased access to western lands, while the Land-Grant College Act (Morrill Act) created the very real possibility that some veterans and their children would have access to higher education.[9] New industries and improved transportation, stimulated by the war, also contained the promise of a better world. As the economic historian Jenny Bourne shows, by 1879 the Northern economy had "caught up" to where it would have been without the war.[10] Bourne notes that in the states that did not secede, "real per capita GDP grew faster after the war than before, with only a small downturn during the financial panic of 1873." Not all parts of the North, or all Northerners, benefited from the war and its aftermath. As Bourne notes, economic inequality increased during and after the war, but the North nevertheless came out of the war on the verge of an economic expansion.

But life was less promising for the defeated soldiers of the traitorous army. Many returned home in tattered uniforms, in ill health, and thoroughly demoralized by their defeat. Their officers faced political disfranchisement and at least the potential of being tried for treason. Many Confederates had committed war crimes by murdering or enslaving captured soldiers. For example, as Foote notes in her chapter, at Dalton, Georgia, Confederates enslaved most of a regiment after it surrendered, which was a war crime under all existing notions of the law of nations, as well as under the military codes of both the Confederate army and the U.S. Army. Many Confederates who had committed war crimes might have faced trials or even executions for their behavior. In the end there was only one war crimes trial, for the barbaric and brutal Henry Wirz, the commander at the Andersonville prison in Georgia. He managed the camp in ways designed to unnecessarily harm the prisoners. For example, he denied them access to clean water, which his own soldiers had and which was readily available. He then ordered his soldiers to shoot prisoners if they reached over makeshift barriers to fill their cups with fresh water. The Wirz trial is generally seen as a failure of due process and the rule of law because of its many procedural irregularities.

---

[9]See Paul Finkelman, "Introduction: The Congress, the Civil War, and the Making of Modern America," in Paul Finkelman and Donald R. Kennon, eds., *Civil War Congress and the Creation of Modern America* (Athens, Ohio, 2018), pp. 1–8.

[10]Goldin and Lewis, "The Economic Cost of the American Civil War," p. 319.

The prosecutors understood the concept of a war crime, and even crimes against humanity, but lacked the necessary legal theory or tools to prosecute Wirz for such crimes. Thus, they tried him for simple murder, and he was convicted and executed. Given the horrible condition of the prisoners—many of whom resembled survivors of Nazi death and concentration camps—Wirz's war crimes were obvious. Lost-cause partisans call his trial an act of vengeance, but in reality it was the world's first modern war crimes trial for crimes against humanity. What is remarkable is not Wirz's conviction but the failure of the United States to try others for war crimes, such as enslaving civilians and POWs or murdering surrendering soldiers.

While U.S. soldiers returned to homes that were mostly untouched by the war, and to an economy that would soon boom, returning Confederates faced devastated cities, factories, and farms. As Bourne notes, the "postbellum South was a wasteland for decades," and this particularly hurt African Americans, 90 percent of whom remained in the South until the twentieth century. At least two or three generations of Southern whites would pay for the treason of their ancestors with poverty and diminished prospects. The economic analysis that shows Northern recovery by 1879 underscores the bleaker future of the South, where "as late as 1909 southerners on average consumed roughly thirty percent less" than they would have if there had been no war.[11] Indeed, given the persistence of poverty in the Deep South, we might argue that some parts of the former Confederacy did not recover from the war until the late twentieth century—or that they still have not recovered.

Thus, when we contemplate the aftermath of the war, we must start with the profound costs for the whole nation, but particularly the South. These human and economic costs are tied to the social and cultural change the war brought—and the cultural and social changes the war failed to accomplish.

The social changes ultimately led to profound legal and constitutional changes. Southern whites almost universally refused to come to terms with black freedom—or even the loss of the war. The postwar Southern governments tried hard to prevent blacks from gaining political power, social rights, or any economic foothold in the postwar society. They tried, as much as possible, to reduce blacks to something close to slavery. Eventually this Southern white obstinacy would lead Congress to pass the Civil Rights Act

---

[11]Ibid.

of 1866 and other laws, as well as to the Fourteenth and Fifteenth amendments. The goal of these amendments and laws was to protect civil rights and suppress white terrorism. These amendments and laws worked for a while, but in the end they were ineffective or ineffectively enforced for more than a century. The essays on the Fourteenth Amendment remind us of its necessity, the process that led to it, and how it was implemented.

The chapters in this book collectively explore some of the ways in which the end of the war continued the trauma of the conflict and also enhanced the potential for the new birth of freedom that Lincoln promised in the Gettysburg Address. We end with Risen's reminder of how the meaning of the war has changed over time, and how the memory has been filtered and remade by a century and a half of myths and serious historical scholarship. While the Civil War is no longer the "felt" history it once was, Risen reminds us that despite the work of many fine scholars, it remains very much a contested history. As we witness continuing conflicts and sometimes lethal disputes over the place of Confederate monuments and Confederate flags in our public space, we realize how much the war is still "felt" in our country, even if the last veterans are now long gone from the debate.

Carole Emberton

"A Hungry Belly and Freedom"

Rations, Refugees, and Reconstruction at the End of the Civil War

T HE SLAVES IN Winnsboro, South Carolina, anticipated the arrival of William Tecumseh Sherman's troops well before they appeared in mid-February 1865. They knew that the state capital of Columbia, just over thirty miles to the south, lay in smoldering ruins. The fleeing residents and retreating Confederate soldiers, who had surrendered on February 17, brought word of the conflagration, and panic spread throughout the up-country plantation districts like the fire that had engulfed the city. While frightened plantation owners worked desperately to bury the family china and silver, to sew heirloom jewelry into the linings of petticoats, and to scatter and hide the scrawny, staggering livestock that remained in the woods and canebrakes, slaves like Savilla Burrell watched and waited with more anticipation than dread. "Us looked for the Yankees on dat place like us look now for de Savior and de host of angels at de second comin'," she recalled. Burrell, who despised the brutal master who sold her siblings away and whipped her mother, believed that the bluecoats brought the fires of atonement with them. Like so many other slaves, she understood the war as divine retribution for the slaves' suffering as well as her own liberation. Her expectations of a joyful deliverance, however, were soon dashed. "Dey come one day in February," she remembered. "De took everything carryable off de plantation and burnt de big house, stables, barns, gin house and dey left the slave houses."[1]

---

[1]Interview with Savilla Burrell, "Born in Slavery: Slave Narratives from the Federal Writers' Project, 1936–1938," Library of Congress, https://memory.loc.gov/ammem /snhtml/snhome.html, accessed June 27, 2016.

That was more than they left Violet Guntharpe, who also lived near Winnsboro. "Well, after ravagin' de whole country side," Guntharpe explained, "de army go across old Catawba [River] and left de air full of de stink of dead carcasses and de sky black wid turkey buzzards." She recalled "de picaninnnies suckin' their thumbs for want of sumpin' to eat." The troops moved on, leaving the newly freed to scavenge for their survival. "Lots of de chillun die," Guntharpe recounted, "as did de old folks, while de rest of us scour de woods for hickory nuts, acorns, cane roots, and artichokes." Barnett Spencer, who had been a slave in Alabama, concurred with Guntharpe's recollections of the hardships of war. Their compliance always controlled through the physical need for food, slaves were accustomed to hunger, but the Union invasion heightened an already meager existence. "The Yankees starved out more black faces than white at their stealing," he remembered. After they came, it was hard to find either food or shelter since many of the buildings on his plantation, including the slave quarters, had been burned. Many ex-slaves "died in piles" from starvation and disease. Hunger left children like Spencer and Guntharpe with an abstract understanding of freedom that was conditional rather than categorical. "De Yankees sho' throwed us in de briar patch . . . all us had to thank them for was a hungry belly, and freedom—[s]umpin' us had no more use for then, than I have today for one of them airplanes I hears flyin' 'round de sky, right now," said Guntharpe. Like the airplanes that hovered high above her, emancipation left only the faintest trail in her life. Her hungry belly, on the other hand, grounded her memories in ways that an abstract concept like freedom could not.[2]

These testimonies given by ex-slaves in the 1930s to the roving bands of interviewers employed through the Federal Writers Project reveal how the most basic of human needs—the need for physical nourishment—tempered the experience of freedom for African Americans across the South. While historians tend to focus on the great boons of formal emancipation, including the granting of national citizenship through the Fourteenth Amendment and the right to vote through the Fifteenth, we tend to avoid the curses that accompanied the wartime expansion of freedom lest we begin to sound too much like the former slave masters who cried incessantly about

---

[2]Interview with Violet Guntharpe, "Born in Slavery: Slave Narratives from the Federal Writers' Project, 1936–1938," Library of Congress, https://memory.loc.gov/ammem /snhtml/snhome.html, accessed June 27, 2016.

the degradation of postemancipation society. Yet the problem of hunger posed a very real threat not only to the lives of vulnerable populations of freedmen and refugees but also to the political reconstruction of the nation. The food crisis facing the postwar South was both a staggering institutional problem and an ideological conundrum that ignited the federal government's long battle with hunger, a battle that continues to this day.

Among the many ghosts that haunted the former Confederacy in the first two years after the war, hunger shadowed the region with a desperate immediacy. Shortly after the surrender, Congress authorized the assistant commissioners of the Bureau of Refugees, Freedmen, and Abandoned Lands (Freedmen's Bureau) to requisition surplus food, clothing, and medicine from local army commanders. In South Carolina, where Violet Guntharpe scoured the woods for food, the bureau began to distribute rations almost immediately; by midsummer, at least 9,000 people had received some 300,000 rations (fig. 1). By the end of the year, the number of rations more than doubled, reaching a total of 25,000 individuals. One year later, it would be nearly a million rations. In 1867—perhaps the leanest and meanest in the postwar period due to crop failures—public and private aid in South Carolina would exceed $300,000.[3]

Similar conditions existed across the South: tens of thousands were left destitute, without adequate food, clothing, or shelter. In Alabama, a mixture of private and public aid distributed nearly four million rations by the autumn of 1866, costing an estimated $643,590. But it was not nearly enough. According to the bureau's assistant commissioner, these figures "did not keep pace with the evidence of suffering." In a report to the secretary of war, he wrote, "At all considerable towns were seen emaciated persons, who had come a long way in quest of food. Letters, newspaper statements, and personal appeals came in from every quarter, while men of prominence and known integrity went to solicit contributions in the north to supplement relief afforded by the government." Even the governor traveled to St. Louis to

---

[3]Martin Abbott, *The Freedmen's Bureau in South Carolina, 1865–1872* (Chapel Hill, N.C., 1967), pp. 37–48. On privation in the Confederacy during the war and its effects on public morale and the Confederate war effort, see William Blair, *Virginia's Private War: Feeding Body and Soul in the Confederacy, 1861–1865* (New York, 2000) and Paul Escott, "'The Cry of the Sufferers': The Problem of Welfare in the Confederacy," *Civil War History* 23 (1977):228–40.

FIG. 1. "Glimpses at the Freedmen's Bureau. Issuing Rations to the old and sick." This illustration in *Frank Leslie's Illustrated Newspaper*, Sept. 22, 1866, depicted African Americans receiving rations from the Freedmen's Bureau office in Richmond, Virginia. *(Library of Congress Prints and Photographs Division)*

bargain for provisions. In the end, he managed to procure 50,000 bushels of corn and "a few hogshead of bacon."[4]

Donations from Northern churches and aid societies, such as the American Union Aid Commission, augmented federal relief, but they could not come close to matching the government's ability to procure, organize, and distribute the staggering amount of relief necessary to alleviate the extreme want in the postwar South. Although accounts are incomplete, a very conservative estimate for the number of federal rations issued by the close of 1866 hovers around twenty million; the cost of those provisions is somewhere in the range of $2 to $3 million. As one historian of the Freedmen's Bureau concluded, "Never before in American history had there been such an organized effort towards such a humanitarian end."[5]

---

[4]"Report of the Assistant Commissioner of Alabama," Sen. Exec. Doc., 39th Cong., 2d sess., vol. 1276, doc. 6, pp. 3–21.
[5]Abbott, *The Freedmen's Bureau in South Carolina*, p. 44.

The relief was not limited to food. Outbreaks of smallpox had made it necessary to burn clothes and bedding and resupply affected communities. The approach of winter left many without warm coats or undergarments. Particularly vulnerable to the elements were freedpeople whose masters had traditionally supplied them with clothing, however limited, at Christmastime. Bitter and burned out, former masters refused to supply their ex-slaves with much of anything, even if they agreed to stay on and work as before. The veil of paternalism stripped away, the bones of the social relationship between black and white were now laid bare. The bureau's agents in South Carolina found the behavior of landowners toward their former bondsmen to be most appalling. According to one agent, "The aged and infirm freedmen were turned out by their former owners, in whose service they had spent their strength, to shift for themselves, and had not this bureau extended aid to them, very many would inevitably have perished on the highways."[6]

Yet hunger and want did not discriminate. Whites, many of them formerly well-to-do, were reduced to begging from the government they so recently warred against. The bureau's agent in Charleston, South Carolina, explained, "Those belonging to the upper classes of society in this city are in actual daily want; the want of capital renders their lands worthless, and there is no sale for that description of property at present." Bureau records make clear that the majority of rations were, in fact, distributed to white refugees. Although initial rules prohibited the distribution of rations to disloyal whites, those restrictions were soon lifted when the depth of the crisis became clear. By the spring of 1866, bureau commissioners instructed their agents to interpret the term "refugee" as liberally as possible and not limit it to those white Unionists who had been driven from their homes by vengeful Confederate neighbors. Thus, Confederate widows and children, along with the most rabid secessionists and even the paroled rebel soldiers, lined up. One has to wonder if the meals made from the government pork, flour, and coffee tasted bitter from the aftertaste of secession, or if the blankets issued by the bureau were able to fend off the chill of defeat. But if Southern

---

[6]"Report of the Assistant Commissioner of South Carolina," Sen. Exec. Doc., 39th Cong., 2d sess., vol. 1276, doc. 6, pp. 112–13. On postwar smallpox epidemics, see James Downs, *Sick from Freedom: African-American Illness and Suffering during the Civil War and Reconstruction* (New York, 2012).

whites feared anything more than starvation, it was equality among the races. They reacted violently to any hint of their former slaves being raised to their level or vice versa. But they were forced to confront their greatest fear in the ration line. "On issuing days might be seen the white lady of respectability standing side by side with the African, both awaiting their turn to receive their weekly supply of rations," reported one bureau official.[7]

Perhaps this was why the government's postwar relief programs received so much criticism. White Southerners, who grew increasingly aggressive in their condemnations of Radical Reconstruction, saw the bureau's ration policy, among its other activities, as encouraging idleness and dependency among the freedpeople, despite the fact that the majority of food relief went to white refugees. Planters argued that relief interfered with the labor market, making freedmen less likely to sign labor contracts because the government would support them. They also charged that bureau agents often sold rations illegally, adding to the growing perception that the organization was corrupt and inefficient. (While there may have been some truth to this in isolated cases, the overwhelming evidence from the bureau's papers suggests that rations were duly and dutifully distributed when available.) To them, the bureau was a "gigantic storehouse" created for the "individual ease and comfort" of freedmen who, so long as the agency existed, would "have nothing to do save to sing and to dance, and to eat the food, and wear the cloths which will be provided for them."[8]

Many Democrats in Congress, as well as moderates within their own party, echoed these charges. President Johnson vetoed the 1866 bill extending the bureau's postwar authority because it was not "consistent with the public welfare." Johnson further explained that "[p]ending the war, many refugees and freedmen received support from the Government, but it was never intended that they should henceforth be fed, clothed, educated, and sheltered by the United States." Congress passed the bill over the president's opposition, but the old bugbear of "dependency" continued to plague efforts to feed the South's vulnerable populations.[9]

---

[7]"Report of the Assistant Commissioner of South Carolina," p. 113.

[8]Abbott, *The Freedmen's Bureau in South Carolina*, p. 121.

[9]"Veto of the Freedmen's Bureau Bill," in Lillian Foster, ed., *Andrew Johnson: His Life and Speeches* (New York, 1866), pp. 232–33.

Perhaps the stiffest and most effective opposition came from within the bureau itself. In June 1865, Captain Charles Soule, the Freedmen's Bureau agent in Orangeburg, South Carolina, called the freedpeople in his district together to "disabuse" them of the "false and exaggerated ideas of freedom" they seemed to possess. "[Y]ou are talking too much; waiting too much; asking for too much," Soule admonished. Irritated by the fact that freedpeople demanded shorter workdays, provisions of food and clothing, shelter, and medical care, Soule warned them that deprivation and suffering were inevitable. Freedom, in fact, might be worse than slavery, at least for a while. He endeavored to explain to the crowd the difference between slavery and freedom as he understood it. "You are now free," he said, "but you must know that the only difference you can feel yet, between slavery and freedom, is that neither you nor your children can be bought or sold. You may have a harder time this year than you have ever had before; it will be the price you pay for your freedom." According to Soule, the line between slavery and freedom was a fine one indeed. The only thing separating the two was the custom of attaching "money value to the former slaves." He found freedpeople's expectations that they should receive some reprieve from the endless work they had endured as slaves outrageous. "If you get through this year alive and well," he told them, "you should be thankful."[10]

Captain Soule was not alone in his belief in the redemptive value of suffering for freedpeople. Fearful that a shortage of labor stemming from former slaves' suspicion of the contract system would endanger agricultural production, Freedmen's Bureau agents throughout the South implemented a variety of coercive policies aimed at reducing dependency on government support and ensuring the freedmen's cooperation with the free labor enterprise. Commissioner Oliver Otis Howard (fig. 2) ordered his assistants to take steps to eliminate "the false pride which renders some of the refugees more willing to be supported in idleness than to support themselves."[11]

---

[10]"To the Freed People of Orangeburg District," June 1865, Letters Received, series 15, Washington Headquarters, Bureau of Refugees, Freedmen, and Abandoned Lands, Record Group 105, National Archives and Records Administration, Washington, D.C. (hereafter NARA).

[11]O. O. Howard, "Circular No. 2," May 19, 1865, Records of the Commissioner, Bureau of Refugees, Freedmen, and Abandoned Lands, RG 105, NARA.

FIG. 2. Oliver Otis Howard from a photograph taken ca. 1861–65. *(Library of Congress Prints and Photographs Division)*

"A Hungry Belly and Freedom" 19

According to many of those agents, the distribution of rations engendered this "false pride," so Howard instructed them to reserve the monthly allotment of one bushel of corn and eight pounds of pork for only the "aged and infirm" and half that amount to very young orphans, both of whom were incapable of labor and self-support. In both of those cases, relatives or caretakers could claim rations for those indigent individuals. All "able-bodied" freedpeople were to be denied assistance in the hope of inducing them to sign contracts and go to work.

Although some agents protested that without rations starvation was certain, Howard assured them in Circular No. 11, issued in August 1865, that "suffering is preferred to slavery, and is, to some degree, the necessary consequences of events." Within a year, Howard would halt all rations except for "the sick in regularly organized hospitals" and children confined to orphan asylums. Because of suspicions that freedpeople were cheating the system and claiming rations for people who could actually work, family and friends could no longer claim assistance for the elderly, sick, and very young living in their homes. While Howard understood his actions as beneficent and integral to the bureau's larger civilizing mission to teach ex-slaves the duties of freedom, the policy gave them a dubious choice: work or starve.[12]

And starve many of them surely did. Even those who worked found themselves unable to break the vicious cycle of debt and dependency that Howard believed could be avoided with enough determination. One South Carolina agent reported a typical case. Twenty-four freedmen contracted to work for a local planter, and at the end of the year, their share of the cotton crop came to $543.43. After deductions for supplies, seven of the men received shares ranging from $4.51 to $8.15 for a year's work. The other seventeen workers ended up owing more than their shares—from $1.71 to $73.62.[13] That was the power and the glory of free labor. Cases such as this one compelled Howard to set aside additional funds in 1867 for rations despite his earlier admonition that only those confined to hospitals or orphanages receive assistance. But many agents continued to blame the freedmen for not managing their money well enough or not spending enough time tending

---

[12]Circular No. 11, Aug. 22, 1865, Select Series of Records Issued by the Commissioner, Bureau of Refugees, Freedmen, and Abandoned Lands, M742, roll 7.

[13]Abbott, *The Freedmen's Bureau in South Carolina*, p. 41.

20 *Carole Emberton*

their crops to ensure a better harvest. Their hard-headedness, the agent at Columbia reported, resulted in "idleness, vagrancy and theft, and was the main cause of half the destitution that existed throughout the District during the year."[14] John W. De Forest, another South Carolina agent who had grown tired of freedpeople's complaints, likewise dismissed their destitution as the inevitable result of their own laziness. "Regular labor is the only thing that will keep you from suffering," he informed the people in his district.[15]

De Forest typified the ambivalence with which many bureau agents viewed their jobs. Reports from the field routinely expressed concern for freedpeople's impoverishment and outrage at the treatment they received at the hands of their former masters but at the same time condemnation for what agents perceived as ignorance, laziness, and dishonesty. De Forest showed particular sympathy for ill-clothed children without proper winter gear and fought to secure clothing, shoes, and blankets from the army. However, he felt rations of food were "demoralizing" and begrudged anything to those he described as "the notoriously idle, the habitual beggars, the thieves, and prostitutes." Recalling the chaos that would erupt on "draw days," when rations were distributed, De Forest derided the "pauper classes" who "made for me like pigs for an oak tree in autumn."[16]

De Forest's hostility toward the poor was not uncommon. As Chad Goldberg notes in his study of social welfare programs in the United States, "Traditional poor relief tended to conflate poverty with deviance and criminality" and often assumed a "rehabilitative function" that could be simultaneously paternalistic and callous. Modern efforts to establish a rational system of government-sponsored social welfare, of which the Freedmen's Bureau was the first, were no less susceptible to the class and racial prejudices of their predecessors. Despite the bureau's attempts to standardize the aid process and the guiding belief that the organization functioned as a protective force that was indispensable to the South's reconstruction, agents like De Forest remained suspicious of certain aspects of the government's intervention, particularly its material support of freedpeople. As a matter of

---

[14]Report of J. D. Greene, Oct. 30, 1866, Select Series of Records Issued by the Commissioner, Bureau of Refugees, Freedmen, and Abandoned Lands, M869, roll 34.

[15]William De Forest, *A Union Officer in the Reconstruction* (Baton Rouge, La., 1997), p. 61.

[16]Ibid., p. 77.

"general principle," De Forest felt it necessary to be "merciless toward the few for the good of the many" by "refusing to feed the suffering lest I encourage the lazy."[17]

If only these antiquated notions of radicalized dependency were actually antiquated. Recent debates in Congress over proposed cuts to the Supplemental Nutrition Assistance Program (SNAP), also known as "food stamps," reveal that Americans' struggle to come to terms with hunger is still ongoing. Representative Stephen Fincher of Tennessee argued that SNAP funding should be drastically reduced by $39 billion because it amounted to nothing less than thievery. "The role of citizens, of Christians, of humanity is to take care of each other," Fincher said, "not for Washington to steal from those in the country and give to others in the country." He then quoted 2 Thessalonians: "The one who is unwilling to work shall not eat." (Never mind that Paul was not referring to taxation or the redistribution of wealth; his letter addressed a group of people who were refusing to work for theological reasons, because they believed the end of time was near.) Fincher's reasoning was historical but not biblical. Combining the argument that government relief is a form of theft and that those who receive aid are categorically lazy and most probably criminals as well (since they are receiving stolen property), Fincher channeled the Reconstruction-era criticisms of food assistance that pilloried attempts to aid a war-torn region and people emerging from a system of forced servitude. Just as it seemed to escape the attention of nineteenth-century opponents of the Freedmen's Bureau that people could *both* work *and* starve, today's critics of government food aid ignore the reality that many of the households receiving public assistance have at least one adult who works full time, yet they remain on the edge of hunger almost daily.[18]

And like their Reconstruction-era counterparts, today's critics of SNAP and other assistance programs cling to a radicalized view of relief that belies the facts. While at least as many white people receive government assistance as blacks—and in the case of SNAP, more whites than blacks receive food assistance—studies reveal that most Americans believe that the

---

[17]Chad Goldberg, *Citizens and Paupers: Relief, Rights, and Race from the Freedmen's Bureau to Workfare* (Chicago, 2008), p. 3; De Forest, *A Union Officer*, p. 60.

[18]Mark Bittman, "Welfare for the Wealthy," *New York Times*, June 4, 2013.

typical "welfare" recipient is black. They also tend to believe that these programs account for a huge portion of the federal budget, when in fact it is less than 1 percent. As Donald Kinder and Cindy Ham wrote in *Us against Them: Ethnocentric Foundations of American Opinion*, "Means-tested programs like AFDC and food stamps are understood by whites to largely benefit shiftless black people." The racialization in perceptions of welfare is reinforced by the news media, which often use images of black people to illustrate stories about welfare and poverty, as Martin Gillens points out in *Why Americans Hate Welfare: Race, Media and the Politics of Antipoverty Policy*. No wonder Nevada rancher Cliven Bundy thinks African Americans were "better off as slaves, when they were picking cotton."[19]

As we commemorate the 150th anniversary of the Civil War, as we celebrate the destruction of chattel bondage, and as we honor the sacrifices of soldiers on the battlefields, let us also remember the suffering that accompanied freedom and the advent of peace. Let us consider the many different ways the war shaped the nation we have become, for better and for worse. The title of the symposium at which the original draft of this chapter was presented, "A Just and Lasting Peace," invokes the idea of justice as articulated by Abraham Lincoln in his second inaugural address. However, when it came to the issue of hunger, it seems that the peace could be *either* just *or* lasting but not both. Too many government officials believed it was not only necessary but also just that freedpeople should suffer and starve in order to learn the lessons of freedom. In this worldview, freedom was a callous, vindictive force that punished instead of protected and left our nation spiritually malnourished.

I would like to end with a meatier vision of justice than the one posed by Lincoln, one that, I think, encompasses the importance of hunger to the lived realities of Americans like Violet Guntharpe, who found that freedom failed to satiate her hungry belly. It is by the Chilean poet Pablo Neruda, from his poem "The Great Tablecloth":

> Let us sit down soon to eat
> with all those who haven't eaten;
> let us spread great tablecloths,

---

[19]Donald Kinder and Cindy Ham, *Us against Them: Ethnocentric Foundations of American Opinion* (Chicago, 2010), p. 199; "A Defiant Rancher Savors the Audience That Rallied at His Side," *New York Times*, Apr. 23, 2014.

put salt in lakes of the world,
set up planetary bakeries,
tables with strawberries in snow,
and a plate like the moon itself
from which we can all eat.

For now I ask no more
than the justice of eating.[20]

---

[20]Pablo Neruda, "The Great Tablecloth," reprinted on The PeaceMeal Project, https://peacemealproject.com/resources-2/poems/, accessed June 27, 2016.

Lorien Foote

Federal Prisoners of War
and the Long Recovery

As the Confederate war effort collapsed in February, March, April, and May 1865, Union officials tried to retrieve the thousands of federal prisoners of war (POWs) still suffering in Confederate prisons. It would prove to be a disordered, tragic, and troublesome process.

Disorder reigned in February and March, when Confederate prison authorities attempted to deliver nearly 8,684 federal prisoners being held in South Carolina to Union military officials in Wilmington, North Carolina. Union forces were at that exact moment engaged in active military operations to capture the city, and the delivery disrupted the Confederate army's defense and hampered the Union's subsequent occupation. To add to the confusion, more than 3,000 federal POWs escaped from Confederate stockades and found their own way to the U.S. Army rather than being returned through a formal exchange process.

Tragedy struck in April. Confederates delivered prisoners from Andersonville in Georgia and Cahaba in Alabama to an exchange point at Vicksburg in Mississippi. Careless and corrupt military officials loaded nearly 2,000 of them onto a wooden-hulled steamer that had just made hasty repairs for leaking boilers. A few miles north of Memphis, Tennessee, on the Mississippi River, the boilers of the overcrowded *Sultana* exploded, killing 1,500 men in the worst maritime disaster in American history (figs. 1 and 2).

Trouble finding federal prisoners who remained in Confederate hands marked both April and May. In some remote locations in the South,

FIG. 1. The steamboat *Sultana*, overcrowded with Union ex-POWs, was photographed on the Mississippi River by Thomas W. Bankes the day before its boilers exploded. *(Library of Congress Prints and Photographs Division)*

FIG. 2. The May 20, 1865, issue of *Harper's Weekly* illustrated the horror of the explosion and sinking of the *Sultana* on April 28, 1865. *(Library of Congress Prints and Photographs Division)*

Confederate camp guards disappeared without telling prisoners that the war was over. It took the Union cavalry until the end of May to find the minor Confederate camps and either liberate the prisoners inside or round up former prisoners running around at large in the vicinity of abandoned prisons.[1]

The United States did not recover all of its POWs until 1866, and federal soldiers liberated themselves throughout 1865. Between May and December, 257 federal prisoners escaped from locations where they were still being held in the states of the former Confederacy. The bulk of these, 240, bolted in May. But former Yankee POWs continued to trickle home in the following months. Ten arrived in June. A soldier who had been captured at Greenleaf Prairie, Oklahoma, reported back to the army in August. Four more arrived in September. In October, three sailors of the Union navy escaped from the vicinity of Camp Ford, Texas. The last recorded federal POW to escape did so in January 1866, when Corporal Henry Scott of the Forty-Fourth United States Colored Troops (USCT) showed up at the camp of the First Iowa Cavalry stationed in Sherman, Texas. He was the last of thirty-two soldiers from his regiment to escape captivity. The colonel of the Forty-Fourth USCT had surrendered his entire garrison at Dalton, Georgia, in October 1864, and Confederates returned many of the enlisted men to slavery. From January to December 1865, thirty-one of them fled from locations in Mississippi, Georgia, and North Carolina. Henry Scott's escape from slavery in Texas, several months after "Juneteenth," marked the end of the Confederate prison system.[2]

---

[1] *Proceedings of the Ohio Association of Union Ex-prisoners of War, at the Reunion Held at Dayton, O., July 29, 30, and 31, 1884, with Register of Members* (Columbus, Ohio, 1884), p. 6; Roger Pickenpaugh, *Captives in Blue: The Civil War Prisons of the Confederacy* (Tuscaloosa, Ala., 2013), pp. 199–200, 224, 225; William Marvel, *Andersonville: The Last Depot* (Chapel Hill, N.C., 1994), pp. 220–28, 234–40; Paul J. Springer and Glenn Robins, *Transforming Civil War Prisons: Lincoln, Lieber, and the Politics of Captivity* (New York, 2015), pp. 23–24; Brian Matthew Jordan, *Marching Home: Union Veterans and Their Unending Civil War* (New York, 2014), pp. 30–31.

[2] Lorien Foote, "Fugitive Federals and the Collapse of the Confederacy," www.Ehistory .org. This database is compiled from the following documents in the National Archives: Federal List of Prisoners Who Escaped, Record Group (RG) 249, Entry 109; Provost Marshal Records from Hilton Head, South Carolina, RG 393, Part I, Entries 4318 and 4294; and Knoxville, Tennessee, RG 249, Entry 32, Box 1; Registrar of Federal Prisoners Who Escaped, RG 249, Entry 31, No. 45; and Letters Received Relating to Union Naval POWs, Reports from Officers and Seamen of the U.S. Navy who were Prisoners of War in the South, RG 45, Entry 56. National Park Service, "The Civil War," http://www.nps.gov /civilwar/search-soldiers-detail.htm?soldierId=61B12FCE-DC7A-DF11-BF36-B8AC6F5 D926A, accessed June 22, 2015; The USCT Chronicle, "What Happened to Private Pryor

FIG. 3. "Serving out rations to our exchanged prisoners of war on board the 'New York,'" sketched by William Waud, *Harper's Weekly*, Dec. 10, 1864. *(Library of Congress Prints and Photographs Division)*

The fiasco at Wilmington, the escape of 3,000 prisoners, and the story of Henry Scott exemplify the challenges of repatriating Civil War prisoners. Processing exchanged, escaped, and liberated POWs posed serious bureaucratic, medical, and humanitarian problems for the federal government, especially because the process often occurred in the midst of the active military operations that ended the war (figs. 3 and 4). Because the process of recovering POWs was chaotic, the consequence for the federal government and Congress was a humanitarian disaster that contributed to demands that Congress recognize the special sufferings of ex-POWs.

The exchange at Wilmington, North Carolina, provides an illustration of the hurdles that prisoners, military officials, doctors, and bureaucrats

---

and the 44th US Colored Infantry?," http://usctchronicle.blogspot.com/2011/02/what-happened-to-private-pryor-and-44th.html, accessed June 22, 2015. It is my surmise that Scott escaped from slavery; federal records do not indicate his escape location. It is a logical conclusion considering the history of the Forty-Fourth USCT and the fact that other African American soldiers were listed as escaping from a "rebel plantation." Camp Ford prison in Texas closed in May and the Tenth Illinois Cavalry burned the remnants of the compound in July 1865. F. E. Lawrence and Robert W. Glover, *Camp Ford C.S.A.: The Story of Union Prisoners in Texas* (Austin, Tex., 1964), pp. 76–79.

FIG. 4. "Our released prisoners at Charleston, S.C., exchanging their rags for new clothing," sketched by William Waud, *Harper's Weekly*, Jan. 14, 1865. *(Library of Congress Prints and Photographs Division)*

faced as the war ended. When U.S. and Confederate officials concluded an agreement in February 1865 to exchange federal POWs being held in South Carolina, a federal joint army-navy operation had recently captured Fort Fisher on the North Carolina coast, the last Confederate stronghold for blockade runners. By February 19, federal forces under the command of Major General John M. Schofield were closing in on the port city of Wilmington from three directions. But neither Schofield nor the Confederate generals defending the city had been informed by their respective governments that federal POWs from South Carolina were being sent their way for exchange. Confederate Major General Robert F. Hoke became discombobulated when 2,500 federal prisoners of war arrived, with thousands more on the way, just as he was trying to move government property from the city in advance of evacuating his garrison. Under a flag of truce, Hoke sent a message to Schofield proposing to deliver the prisoners immediately. Since Schofield was unaware of any exchange agreement and did not want anything to impede his advance, he asked the Confederate general for more

Federal Prisoners of War and the Long Recovery 29

information about the terms of delivery and continued to press toward Wilmington with his troops. The beleaguered Hoke sent panicked dispatches to Confederate prison officials ordering them not to send any more prisoners to Wilmington. He sent staff officers to the front lines to impress on commanders the necessity of delaying the federal advance in order to gain time to remove the prisoners.[3]

The result was chaos and humanitarian disaster. Hoke sent the prisoners to Goldsboro, North Carolina, where they were turned out into an open field with no shelter. Transporting the federals out of Wilmington took up the train cars that were supposed to evacuate Confederate naval stores. Confederate prison officials and railroad managers had no idea where to put thousands of other prisoners who were on their way to Wilmington, who could not now be delivered, and ended up moving them back and forth between points on the railroad at Salisbury, Greensboro, Raleigh, and Goldsboro, consuming the transportation that was needed to move military supplies. At least 2,500 of these prisoners were severely ill from exposure and malnourishment. Three hundred and sixty of them were put in a makeshift hospital on the fairgrounds outside of Goldsboro. Confederate prison officials, no strangers to the suffering of federal prisoners, reported that the "neglect, filth, and squalor" of this place was unequaled in their experience. It was a "state of affairs that I felt disgraced our character for humanity," admitted Colonel Henry Forno, the officer in charge of moving federal prisoners out of South Carolina.[4]

Early on the morning of February 22, Confederate forces evacuated Wilmington and withdrew across the Northeast Cape Fear River, abandoning

---

[3]Maj. Gen. R. F. Hoke to Gen. B. T. Johnson, Feb. 20, 1865, Maj. Gen. R. F. Hoke to Maj. Parker, Feb. 20, 1865, and Maj. Gen. J. M. Schofield to Maj. Gen. R. F. Hoke, Feb. 21, 1865, in *The War of the Rebellion: A Compilation of the Official Records of the Union and Confederate Armies* (Washington, D.C., 1880–1901), ser. 2, vol. 8, pp. 276, 286 (hereafter *O.R.*); Chris E. Fonvielle Jr., *The Wilmington Campaign: Last Rays of Departing Hope* (Campbell, Calif., 1997), pp. 393–414; Johnson Hagood, *Memoirs of the War of Secession* (Columbia, S.C., 1910), pp. 342–43.

[4]Col. H. Forno to Brig. Gen. Johnson, Feb. 22, 1865, Gen. L. S. Baker to Gen. Johnson, Feb. 22, 1865, Brig. Gen. L. S. Baker to Lt. Gen. Braxton Bragg, Feb. 21, 1865, Col. H. Forno to Asst. Adj. Gen. Brig. Gen. Gardner's Staff, Mar. 10, 1865, in *O.R.*, ser. 2, vol. 8, pp. 288, 294, 378; Duncan McKercher Pocket Diary, Feb. 27–28, 1865, HM48562, Huntington Library, San Marino, Calif.; Leon Basile, ed., *The Civil War Diary of Amos E. Stearns, a Prisoner at Andersonville* (East Brunswick, N.J., 1981), p. 113; A. O. Abbott, *Prison Life in the South: At Richmond, Macon, Savannah, Charleston, Columbia, Charlotte, Raleigh, Goldsborough, and Andersonville, during the Years 1864 and 1865* (New York, 1865), pp. 179–80.

30 *Lorien Foote*

200 federal prisoners who had escaped and hidden for three days in the swamps and woods around Wilmington, waiting for federal forces to capture the city. The advance units of the Union army, including the Third New Hampshire and the Seventh Connecticut, encountered these escaped prisoners as they emerged from their hiding places, or found them dead along the road. Hoke, from his position in the field across the river, contacted Schofield again and urged him "in the name of humanity" to accept the delivery of the federal prisoners waiting at Goldsboro and other points. "They have been subjected to great suffering and considerable mortality by the delay," he pointed out. On February 23, firmly in command of Wilmington, Schofield agreed to halt active operations along the Northeast Cape Fear River and to receive 2,000 prisoners a day, beginning on February 26.[5]

Between February 26 and March 4, Confederate officials delivered 8,684 federal POWs to the exchange point at a railroad crossing on the Northeast Cape Fear River.[6] From the moment of their arrival, Union medical officials scrambled to appropriately address the returned prisoners' medical needs. Regiments stationed at the Northeast Cape Fear River, on order from Schofield, had prepared a feast with plenty of strong coffee for the famished prisoners, who mobbed the cooking kettles and devoured as much food as they could get their hands on. When the prisoners arrived at Wilmington, federal soldiers stationed in the city also fed them, and initially the federal commissary distributed sugar, meat, onions, soft bread, and hardtack. "We drank the army coffee until we were filled, and still its delicious fragrance filled the air and intoxicated our senses," wrote one former prisoner. "I drank

---

[5]Maj. Gen. R. F. Hoke to Commanding General U.S. Forces, Wilmington, Feb. 22, 1865, Lt. Gen. U. S. Grant to Lt. Col. Mulford, Feb. 26, 1865, Special Orders 12, Headquarters Department of North Carolina, Army of the Ohio, Feb. 23, 1865, in *O.R.*, ser. 2, vol. 8, pp. 290, 310, 296; Daniel Eldredge, *The Third New Hampshire and All about It* (Boston, 1893), p. 636; Stephen Walkley, *History of the Seventh Connecticut Volunteer Infantry, Hawley's Brigade, Terry's Division, Tenth Army Corps, 1861–1865* (Southington, Conn., 1905), pp. 196–99; Sidney S. Williams, "From Spotsylvania to Wilmington, N.C. by Way of Andersonville and Florence," in *Personal Narratives of Events in the War of the Rebellion, Being Papers Read before the Rhode Island Soldiers and Sailors Historical Society*, Fifth Series, No. 10 (Providence, R.I., 1899), pp. 44–45.

[6]Brevet Brig. Gen. Joseph C. Abbott to Maj. J. A. Campbell, Mar. 5, 1865, Cpt. J. Louis Smith to Inspector General Samuel Cooper, Mar. 31, 1865, in *O.R.*, ser. 2, vol. 8, pp. 358, 449–50; Walkley, *History of the Seventh Connecticut*, p. 200; Henry F. W. Little, *The Seventh New Hampshire Volunteers in the War of the Rebellion* (Concord, N.H., 1896), pp. 412–16; Benjamin F. Booth and Steve Meyer, *Dark Days of the Rebellion: Life in Southern Military Prisons* (Garrison, Iowa, 1995), p. 226.

so much of it that I was positively and helplessly drunk." Others became desperately ill as their famished and debilitated stomachs rejected the food. Too late for many prisoners, who suffered the consequences of the orgy of eating for weeks, army physicians intervened. They watched over the prisoners to keep them from overeating and ordered the commissary to issue limited rations four times a day to keep the returned prisoners from eating their food all at once, a temptation that proved impossible to resist.[7]

Because the prisoner exchange took place during an active military campaign, there had been no preparation to receive the prisoners. The arrival of 8,684 captives exhausted local resources and military supply lines and threatened the health of the community. Caring for the POWs hindered the federal army's ability to occupy and stabilize Wilmington. The majority of the prisoners were forwarded by steamer within a few days to Camp Parole in Annapolis, Maryland, but 2,475 were too sick to be moved for several weeks. Several hundred of these prisoners died before they could be removed from the city; deaths averaged seventeen a day. Military commanders had to improvise and provide ad hoc care. Warehouses were converted to hospitals, and citizens took men into their homes. Major General Alfred H. Terry diverted shoes and clothing intended for Major General William Tecumseh Sherman's army to the paroled prisoners, and was therefore unable to immediately supply Sherman when his army arrived in North Carolina. The emergency was not alleviated until March 19, when the United States Sanitary Commission arrived to take charge of the prisoners, bringing a steamer from New York City with enough food (including 3,300 pounds of chocolate), clothing, and medical supplies to adequately care for the sick prisoners. Ultimately, caring for returned POWs delayed the advance of the Union troops out of the city for their intended rendezvous with Sherman's army.[8]

---

[7]Maj. William M. Wherry to Maj. Gen. A. H. Terry, Feb. 23, 1865, in *O.R.*, ser. 2, vol. 8, p. 297; B. F. Travis, *Story of the 25th Michigan* (Kalamazoo, Mich., 1897), p. 342; Walkley, *History of the Seventh Connecticut*, p. 201; Booth and Meyer, *Dark Days of the Rebellion*, p. 227; Basile, *Diary of Amos Stearns*, p. 115.

[8]Fonvielle, *The Wilmington Campaign*, pp. 446–50; Brig. Gen. A. F. Terry to William T. Sherman, Mar. 13, 1865, Joseph R. Hawley to Col. J. A. Campbell, Mar. 20, 1865, in *O.R.*, ser. 1, vol. 42, part 2, pp. 818–19, 926–27; Paul Murray and Stephen Russell Bartlett Jr., "The Letters of Stephen Chaulker Bartlett Aboard the U.S.S. 'Lenapee,' January to August 1865," *North Carolina Historical Review* 33, no. 1 (Jan. 1956):82; U.S. Sanitary Commission, *No. 87: Preliminary Report of the Operations of the U.S. Sanitary Commission in North*

32   *Lorien Foote*

Prisoners who returned to Union lines, no matter when or where, faced an extended journey home that usually lasted weeks. The three enemies of a short passage were convoluted transportation routes, government bureaucracy, and the wasted bodies of the liberated prisoners. Escaped prisoner Chauncy S. Aldrich spent seven days in Washington, D.C., trying to obtain his necessary paperwork. He visited the adjutant general's office, spent two full days sitting in the Quartermaster's Department, and finished with an examination by auditors who finally issued the necessary certificates for him to visit the paymaster. His terse diary entry summarized his feelings: "Got very much vexed."[9]

Benjamin Booth's journey from Wilmington to his home in Iowa exemplified the physical and mental endurance necessary to transform out of the condition of being a POW. The government provided aid for only part of the journey, which contributed to Booth's physical decline. The federal steamship *Sunshine* transported Booth from Wilmington to Camp Parole, Maryland, a processing station for returned prisoners (fig. 5). There, military officials lined up the ex-prisoners of war, issued a complete suit of clothes, and marched them en masse to the bath house to an assembly line for cleanliness that was so efficient it took ten minutes per person. The returned prisoners were stripped naked, had their heads shaved to remove lice, were scrubbed in the bath by two strong men, were wiped dry with coarse towels by two others, and were passed to the final room, where they put on their new clothes. After his cleansing, Booth filled out paperwork and received twenty-five cents a day for every day he was in prison; the pay was for rations he did not receive from the Union army while he was incarcerated in Confederate prisons.

The government provided transportation for part of Booth's journey from Annapolis to his home in Iowa. Trains took Booth on an eight-day journey through Baltimore, Columbus, and Indianapolis to Benton Barracks in St. Louis. The trip was difficult because of Booth's extreme physical weakness. His digestive system was a wreck. "To me, everything eatable is loathsome, yet I am hungry all the time," he wrote of the common

---

Carolina, March, 1865, and upon the Physical Condition of Exchanged Prisoners Lately Received at Wilmington, N.C. (New York, 1865), pp. 3–9, 17.

[9] "Army Life and Prison Experiences of Major Charles G. Davis," Special Collections, University of Tennessee-Knoxville Libraries; C.S. Aldrich, Civil War Diary, SM1, Folder 1, Chauncy S. Aldrich Collection, Pritzker Military Museum and Library, Chicago.

FIG. 5. Camp Parole, Annapolis, Maryland, in a print issued by E. Sachse and Co. in May 1865. *(Library of Congress Prints and Photographs Division)*

symptom experienced by returned prisoners that lasted for months after the war: an insatiable desire to eat accompanied by the inability to eat. His desire to get home obsessed his mind and turned minutes into weeks. He hid his burning fever from the doctor so he would not have to go to the hospital.

Booth reached Iowa City on March 18. He had not eaten for two days. In some cities, local charity organizations provided soldiers' rest stations for returned POWs with food, a place to stay, and information to ease the transition. Booth found no such help. The government did not provide transportation for the final twenty-five miles of his journey from the train station to his home. He and a comrade hired a ride and stopped at a farmhouse for dinner ten miles from his home. There Booth collapsed, "powerless to move." The kind lady of the house offered her bed, but Booth refused because he still had vermin crawling on him, despite his cleansing in Annapolis. He lay on the ground and writhed in pain. The next morning his wife and brother-in-law arrived to take him home in a wagon. For the next three weeks Booth was delirious and unconscious, unable to recognize the wife who nursed him day and night. Although he had reached home in March, Booth was not able to record his homecoming in his diary until December 20, 1865.[10]

---

[10]Booth, *Dark Days of the Rebellion*, pp. 233–43; Austin A. Carr, *Three Years Cruise of Austin A. Carr in Co. F 2nd N.Y.S.M. or 82nd N.Y. Vol. Second Division, Second Corps, Army of the*

34 Lorien Foote

There were more than 164,525 former POWs in the North after the war, and Congress faced the consequences of their physical devastation. The belief that the Confederate leadership and its minions deliberately and systematically abused federal prisoners was pervasive in the North and played a critical role in postwar politics. The Northern public was saturated with stories of atrocities and starvation that appeared regularly in the press and in congressional reports. Andersonville in particular, and federal POWs in general, became the overarching symbol used in the North to represent the barbarity of the rebellion. Congressmen debating plans for Reconstruction in 1866 referred to reports about Confederate prisons to justify their proposed programs; the Republican Party's 1868 election campaign continually referenced Andersonville and images of Confederate stockades. The initiation ritual for the Grand Army of the Republic, the politically powerful veterans' organization, involved dressing the initiate as a POW and marching him past a coffin labeled with the name and regiment of a soldier who died at Andersonville. The House of Representatives investigated the treatment of federal POWs in 1869 and concluded that atrocities were the "inevitable results" of slavery, treason, and rebellion. Historians have suggested that bitterness over this issue obstructed reconciliation between Northerners and Southerners through the decade of the 1870s. The historian of one of the Union regiments that witnessed the exchange at the Northeast Cape Fear River encapsulated in 1885 the lingering anger. Even though Northern and Southern soldiers now meet in fraternal friendship, he wrote, the deliberate abuse of prisoners "is a crime never to be forgotten nor forgiven."[11]

Potomac, Huntington Library, San Marino, Calif.; W. F. Lyon, *In and out of Andersonville* (Detroit, Mich., 1905); Alfred S. Roe, "Richmond, Annapolis, and Home," in *Personal Narratives of Events in the War of the Rebellion, Being Papers Read before the Rhode Island Soldiers and Sailors Historical Society*, Fourth Series, No. 17 (Providence, R.I., 1892), pp. 29–30.

[11]U.S. House of Representatives, 38th Cong., 1st sess., Report No. 67, Joint Committee on the Conduct and Expenditures of the War, "Report: Returned Prisoners," May 9, 1864, Huntington Library, San Marino, Calif.; *Narrative of Privations and Sufferings of United States Officers and Soldiers While Prisoners of War in the Hands of the Rebel Authorities: Being the Report of a Commission of Inquiry, Appointed by the United States Sanitary Commission* (Boston, 1864); Benjamin G. Cloyd, *Haunted by Atrocity: Civil War Prisons in American Memory* (Baton Rouge, La., 2010), pp. 24–45; Stuart McConnell, *Glorious Contentment: The Grand Army of the Republic, 1865–1900* (Chapel Hill, N.C., 1992), pp. 93–94; B. F. Thompson, *History of the 112th Regiment of Illinois Volunteer Infantry in the Great War of the Rebellion, 1862–1865* (Toulan, Ill., 1885), p. 310. Brian Matthew Jordan

Most former POWs never fully recovered from their captivity, even when they enjoyed a generally fulfilling life after the war. Physical ailments plagued them until death, and sharp, clear, unwanted memories of life in prison were deeply embedded in their minds. Modern science suggests that biochemical reactions produced during traumatic experiences cause persistent, detailed, and intrusive memories of the event. One former POW wrote that his experience "did not leave a misty impression upon the mind, but is eaten into the imagination as if by an acid—etched indelibly upon the memory." Union ex-POWs became a distinct and honored subset of veterans whose claim to have endured the greatest suffering and sacrifice for the cause of any Union soldier was conceded to them by other veterans and by the Northern public.[12]

Because former POWs claimed to have endured unique and long-lasting suffering, they demanded that Congress automatically grant a pension to any man who could prove that he was confined in a Confederate prison during the war. This demand took place in the context of a national debate over federal pensions for veterans. In order to reward and care for citizens who fought to save the Union, Congress had passed a series of ever more liberal and expansive pension laws between 1861 and 1879 that incorporated increasing numbers of veterans into their provisions. Applicants for pensions had to prove that they suffered a disability owing to wounds or disease that was a direct result of their military service. Proponents of liberal pensions argued that the nation owed this debt to veterans who had sacrificed their health, rather than their lives, to save the Union. Opponents feared the drain on the Treasury, accused the Pension Bureau of corruption and fraud, and

---

argues that at the end of the 1860s the Northern public was tired of the POW issue and that ex-POWs no longer had a friendly audience for their tales. They became bitter, more vocal, and more unable to heal as the rest of society tried to move on. See Jordan, *Marching Home*, pp. 130–34.

[12] A. H. Hazelett, "Prison Life, East and West," in *War Sketches and Incidents as Related by the Companions of the Iowa Commandery, Military Order of the Loyal Legion of the United States* (Des Moines, Iowa, 1898), 2:388; G. E. Sabre, *Nineteen Months a Prisoner of War: Narrative of Lieutenant G.E. Sabre, Second Rhode Island Cavalry, of His Experience in the War Prisons and Stockades of Morton, Mobile, Atlanta, Libby, Belle Island, Andersonville, Macon, Charleston, and Columbia, and His Escape to the Union Lines* (New York, 1865), p. 9; Barbara A. Gannon, *The Won Cause: Black and White Comradeship in the Grand Army of the Republic* (Chapel Hill, N.C., 2011), pp. 10, 125; Jordan, *Marching Home*, p. 73; James Marten, *Sing Not War: The Lives of Union and Confederate Veterans in Gilded Age America* (Chapel Hill, N.C., 2011), pp. 268–69.

36   *Lorien Foote*

worried that liberal pension laws undermined the manly independence of veterans.[13]

Former POWs joined associations that lobbied Congress to recognize them as a special class of veteran. These organizations served multiple purposes in helping ex-POWs navigate their long recovery. Meetings served as a place where they could share the powerful memories they endured; they began by singing prison songs, and then each veteran had the opportunity to share some of his experiences. Constitutions for such organizations proclaimed the intent of preserving a historical record of the causes of the war, the true character of Confederate prisons, and the sufferings endured by their inmates. Members pledged to cultivate a spirit of forgiveness toward their torturers and to share their resources with destitute comrades. Former POWs produced an abundance of prison narratives that described the horrors of Confederate prison, proclaimed that suffering in prison was as noble and heroic as battlefield wounds, and demanded that the public acknowledge that prisoners played a central role in the Union victory.[14]

Felix LaBaume, the president of the National Ex-Prisoners of War Association, sent just such a message to Congress in one of the numerous petitions that flowed into that body. He pointed out that the U.S. government decided not to exchange prisoners during 1863 and 1864 so that healthy Confederate POWs would not be able to return to the front lines and fight. Therefore, he argued, Union POWs played an active part in the war by being confined in prison; they helped end it sooner than it would have otherwise ended. But many former prisoners could not secure pensions because of flaws in the law regarding evidence: they could not secure a surgeon's affidavit either because U.S. surgeons had not examined them or because their physical symptoms did not fall under the categories covered by the laws. "It should be clear by now that all former prisoners of war were permanently disabled by being in prison," LaBaume exhorted the members of Congress.[15]

---

[13]John William Oliver, *History of the Civil War Military Pensions, 1861–1885*, Bulletin of the University of Wisconsin, No. 844, History Series, 4, no. 1 (Madison, Wis., 1917), pp. 35–71.

[14]*Proceedings of the Ohio Association of Union Ex-prisoners of War*, pp. 5–12; "Prison Experience of Maj. Charles G. Davis"; John L. Ransom, *Andersonville Diary, Escape, and List of the Dead, with Name, Co., Regiment, Date of Death and No. of Grave in Cemetery* (Auburn, N.Y., 1881), pp. 189–99; Cloyd, *Haunted by Atrocity*, p. 65.

[15]*Proceedings of the Ohio Association of Union Ex-prisoners of War*, pp. 5–12; "Prison Experience of Maj. Charles G. Davis"; Ransom, *Andersonville Diary*, pp. 189–99.

Congressmen responded with two proposals to provide pensions to all former POWs. In 1880 during the Forty-Sixth Congress, Representative Joseph Warren Keifer of Ohio, who had been a major general of volunteers during the war and would serve as Speaker of the House for the Forty-Seventh Congress, introduced HR 4495 to represent the demands of his 1,500 constituents who were members of the Ohio Association of Union Ex-Prisoners of War. Echoing LaBaume's language, the proposed bill stated that all POWs were permanently injured but their debilities often were too general and indefinable to be covered under existing law. The bill required the government to place on the pension rolls all men who were confined for more than six months in a Confederate prison and to pay eight dollars a month to those men who were confined for six months to a year. Any former POW who was confined for longer than a year would get an additional dollar for every additional month of his confinement. When this bill failed, Ohio Representative James S. Robinson introduced a more liberal bill, HR 5968, in the Forty-Seventh Congress. Former POWs who were confined for two to six months would get a half pension, those confined for six to twelve months would get a three-quarter pension, and those in prison for twelve months would receive a full pension. In addition, ex-POWs would receive two dollars a day for every single day they spent in a Confederate prison. As the historian Brian Matthew Jordan has pointed out, this legislation would have written into law the "harrowing consequences of captivity" and deemed mental injuries "worthy and heroic."[16]

Despite four efforts to secure passage of these and similar bills during the 1880s, they failed. Not all Americans conceded that confinement in Confederate prisons created an automatic disability that lasted for life. Democrats in Congress, many of whom were former Confederates, worried about economy in government spending and the sectional bitterness such proposals stimulated. Former POWs did not have their special sufferings encoded as they wished. But survivors who lived to 1890 did receive a pension. In that year, Congress passed the Dependent Pension Act, which granted a pension to

---

[16]Ransom, *Andersonville Diary*, pp. 189–99; *Proceedings of the Ohio Association of Union Ex-prisoners of War*, pp. 13–14; Jordan, *Marching Home*, pp. 148–49, 274; History, Art & Archives: United States House of Representatives, "Keifer, Joseph Warren," http://history .house.gov/People/Detail/16140, accessed Apr. 2, 2015; History, Art & Archives: United States House of Representatives, "Robinson, James Sidney," http://history.house.gov/People /Detail/20503?ret=True, accessed Apr. 2, 2015.

38   *Lorien Foote*

any disabled veteran who was honorably discharged after at least ninety days of service. The veteran did not need to prove that his disability was incurred during military service. By 1893, the federal government was devoting 43 percent of its expenditures to pensions.[17]

Federal soldiers who were confined in Confederate prisons faced a long process of repatriation that extended across the months and years after the war and a long personal recovery that lasted for decades. In 1889, the last federal POW returned to his home. John B. Hotchkiss had escaped from Andersonville prison during the war and headed to Florida. But illness induced amnesia. Residents of a small coastal town found him compulsively trying to board any vessel heading out to sea. He could not identify himself or explain his intentions. The villagers thought he was crazy. Eventually he reached Key West and lived and worked there as John Schooner. One day Hotchkiss read an obituary in the newspaper about a man killed in Brooklyn, New York. The widow's brother had disappeared during the war but she never lost faith that she would recover him. The article triggered his memory and his realization of his identity. He was John Hotchkiss, escaped POW, and he was finally free.[18]

---

[17]Marten, *Sing Not War*, p. 17; Jordan, *Marching Home*, p. 149.
[18]Marten, *Sing Not War*, p. 226.

Jenny Bourne

When Johnny Came Marching Home, What Did He Find?

A Look at the Postbellum U.S. Economy

THE CIVIL WAR radically changed the role of the federal government in the macroeconomy. It also cost a lot: per capita federal debt in 1859 was less than two dollars but rose to over seventy-six dollars by 1865.[1] Once the war ended, so did government payouts for men and matériel. That withdrawal, coupled with the need to repay government creditors, might seem to set the stage for recession. In fact, real per capita GDP grew faster after the war than before, with only a small downturn during the financial panic of 1873.[2]

But the fruits of growth did not fall evenly. What little data we have indicate an increase in wealth inequality throughout the nineteenth century. Postbellum farm productivity lagged relative to overall productivity, and the new industrial economy brought terrible workplace conditions for ordinary laborers. Most notably, the postbellum South was a wasteland for decades,

---

[1]Susan B. Carter, Scott Sigmund Gartner, Michael R. Haines, Alan L. Olmstead, Richard Sutch, and Gavin Wright, eds., *Historical Statistics of the United States, Earliest Times to the Present: Millennial Edition* (New York, 2006), http://dx.doi.org/10.1017/ISBN -9780511132971.A.ESS.01, Series Ea650–51.

[2]Willard Thorp, writing during World War II, noted that depressions typically follow wars when the government withdraws as a customer for military goods and services. Willard Thorp, "Postwar Depressions," *American Economic Review* 30 (1941):352–61. Thorp's work suggested a need for postwar planning. Depression did not occur after the Civil War; because of booming economic conditions, per capita federal debt actually halved between 1866 and 1880. Carter et al., *Historical Statistics*, Series Ea650–51.

39

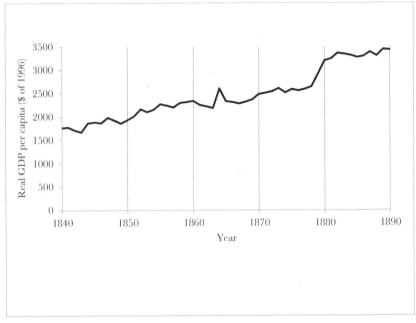

FIG. 1. Real GDP per capita, 1840–90. Source: Carter et al., *Historical Statistics*, Series Ca16.

particularly for black Americans—nine-tenths of whom remained below the Mason-Dixon Line in 1900.[3]

Overall Growth and Its Components

Figure 1 shows the upward climb in real GDP per capita from 1840 to 1890. Annualized growth rates tell a more nuanced story: the rate was 1.65 percent in the two decades before the Civil War but rose to 1.89 percent in the years after the war up to 1890.[4]

---

[3]Carter et al., *Historical Statistics*, Series Ac43; Steven Ruggles, J. Trent Alexander, Katie Genadek, Ronald Goeken, Matthew B. Schroeder, and Matthew Sobek, *Integrated Public Use Microdata Series: Version 5.0* (Minneapolis, 2010) [machine-readable database].

[4]I fit an exponential function to estimate the annual rates for each period. The annualized growth rate in real GDP per capita was 1.15 percent during the Civil War. The data before 1840 are spotty, but estimates indicate an annualized growth rate of 0.73 percent for the period 1790 to 1840. Paul Rhode and Richard Sutch, "Estimates of National Product before 1929," in Carter et al., *Historical Statistics*. Growth was below trend

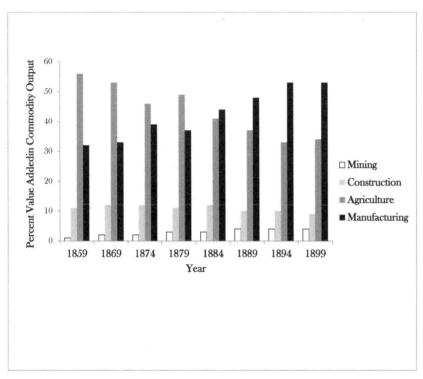

FIG. 2. Sectoral production, 1859–99. Source: Robert Gallman, "Commodity Output, 1839–1899," in *Trends in the American Economy in the Nineteenth Century* (Princeton, N.J., 1960), p. 26.

Why? Because productivity increased: a given amount of inputs yielded a greater quantity of output than before. This was true for both manufacturing and agriculture, although productivity growth was markedly greater in industry. And industry mattered more by the mid-1880s, as figure 2 shows.

---

in the half decade following the financial panic of 1873, which began the third week of September and was followed by an industrial downturn. The trigger for the 1873 panic, like the one for the panic of 1857, was excessive lending to railroad companies. One of the victims of the 1873 panic was Jay Cooke and Company, which had offered large advances to the Northern Pacific Railroad. Warren Persons, Pierson Tuttle, and Edwin Frickey, "Business and Financial Conditions following the Civil War in the United States," *Review of Economics and Statistics* 2 (1920):5–21. Joseph Davis, "An Annual Index of US Industrial Production 1790–1915," *Quarterly Journal of Economics* 119 (2004):1177–215, uses physical volume data on forty-three manufacturing and mining industries to suggest that the downturn after the panic of 1873 was shorter lived and milder than earlier scholars had thought.

42   *Jenny Bourne*

Productivity growth was fueled in part by hardworking new Americans. Immigration to the United States exploded because of the opening of cheap fertile land to the west, with a net 2.2 million people arriving during the 1870s and 4.7 million during the next decade.[5] Extensive railroad growth aided the westward movement. In 1860, 31,000 miles of main-line track were in operation. This figure climbed to 74,000 by 1875 and 167,000 by 1890.[6]

Not only did railroads expand, but early in the 1870s the country replaced its iron rails with steel, which has significantly greater load-bearing capability.[7] This meant immense savings on transportation costs. In 1868, the cost to send a bushel of wheat from Chicago to New York was 30.49 cents; by 1898 the cost had fallen to 1.55 cents.[8]

Lawmakers set the stage for western growth during the Civil War, with 1862 being an especially busy year. The Thirty-Seventh Congress passed the Homestead Act on May 20 and authorized a transcontinental railroad on July 1, encouraging the population of the trans-Mississippi West to swell from 4.5 million in 1860 to 16.4 million in 1900.[9]

One indicator of progress is the amount of patent activity. Figure 3 shows its escalation after the Civil War, in part due to war-related inventions. The United States issued half a million patents from 1860 to 1890 and became the world leader in applied technology.[10]

---

[5]Carter et al., *Historical Statistics*, Series Ad22. Persons et al., "Business and Financial Conditions," point to the steady and rapid increase in national output, the surplus revenue of the government, and the increasing immigration to the United States as evidence of a quick recovery from the Civil War.

[6]Carter et al., *Historical Statistics*, Series Df884.

[7]Jacob Conner, "Industrial Causes Affecting American Commercial Policy Since the Civil War," *Annals of American Academy of Political and Social Sciences* 23 (1904):43–54. Railroads expanded in the South as well. Maury Klein, "Southern Railroad Leaders 1865–1893: Identities and Ideologies," *Business History Review* 42 (1968):288–310.

[8]Conner, "Industrial Causes." Some of the decline was due to general deflation, but most was true savings.

[9]Sidney Ratner, James Soltow, and Richard Sylla, *The Evolution of the American Economy: Growth, Welfare, and Decision Making*, 2nd ed. (New York, 1993), p. 259. Overall U.S. population doubled from 1860 to 1890 and tripled from 1860 to 1910. Carter et al., *Historical Statistics*, Series Aa2. On the same day as it blessed the transcontinental railroad, Congress established the Internal Revenue Service and outlawed bigamy. The next day, it passed the Land-Grant College Act. Congress in 1862 also made fiat money legal tender and freed slaves in the District of Columbia and the territories. Legislative bodies can be amazingly active when the dissidents have departed!

[10]Persons et al., "Business and Financial Conditions"; John Hope Franklin, *From Slavery to Freedom*, 6th ed. (New York, 1988), p. 202; Nathan Rosenberg, *Perspectives on Technology* (New York, 1976).

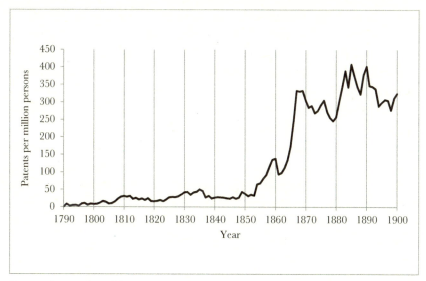

FIG. 3. Patents issued for inventions, 1790–1900. Source: Carter et al., *Historical Statistics*, Series Aa9, Cg30.

Distribution of the Fruits of Growth

Although information about personal wealth during the nineteenth century is sketchy, the best estimates indicate that the wealthy were getting wealthier.[11] The top 20 percent of households possessed just under three-quarters of wealth in 1820 but owned over 97 percent by 1900. In part, this trend occurred because of the unusual amount of equality that existed in the colonies.[12]

Some of the wealthy bear familiar names: Andrew Carnegie (who was superintendent of military railroads and telegraph lines during the Civil War

---

[11]Jeffrey Williamson, "Inequality, Accumulation and Technological Imbalance: A Growth-Equity Conflict in American History?," *Economic Development and Cultural Change* 27 (1979):231–53; Jeffrey Williamson and Peter Lindert, *American Inequality: A Macroeconomic History* (New York, 1980); Richard Steckel and Carolyn Moehling, "Rising Inequality: Trends in the Distribution of Wealth in Industrializing New England," *Journal of Economic History* 61 (2001):160–83; Jeremy Atack, Fred Bateman, and Robert Margo, "Skill Intensity and Rising Wage Dispersion in Nineteenth-Century American Manufacturing," *Journal of Economic History* 64 (2004):172–92.

[12]Peter Lindert, "The Distribution of Income and Wealth," in Carter et al., *Historical Statistics*.

44 Jenny Bourne

and supervised the evacuation of the Union army after First Bull Run), Jay Cooke (who, with Lincoln's gratitude, generated effective ways to market government bonds directly to the public during the war), and John D. Rockefeller (who was an abolitionist supporter of Lincoln but hired surrogates to fight in his place). Some call these men "robber barons," but others note they succeeded largely because they adopted efficient technology and innovative methods.[13]

The Gilded Age had other success stories, however. From having nothing in 1865, one-fifth of black farm operators actually owned their land by 1880.[14] The wealth of black Georgians grew 9 percent annually from 1875 to 1892.[15] Of course, blacks' income and wealth remained substantially below that of whites; but, in some ways, the achievements of newly freed blacks outshone those of the white men at the top. Still, wealth generally became more unequally distributed.

Monetary Policy, Price Changes, Creditors, and Debtors

One factor contributing to the unevenness of growth was money market activity during the Civil War and Reconstruction. To finance the war, the nation moved from commodity money (backed by gold and silver) to fiat money (backed by nothing other than the full faith and credit of the federal government).[16] Although the United States operates with fiat money now, it was a major innovation in the 1860s.

---

[13] Ellis Oberholtzer, *Jay Cooke: Financier of the Civil War*, 2 vols. (Philadelphia, 1907); Allan Nevins, *Study in Power: John D. Rockefeller, Industrialist and Philanthropist*, 2 vols. (New York, 1953); Ron Chernow, *Titan: The Life of John D. Rockefeller Sr.* (New York, 1998); David Nasaw, *Andrew Carnegie* (New York, 2006); Jenny Bourne, "To Slip the Surly Bonds of State Rights and Form a More Perfect (Financial) Union: One Legacy of the Thirty-Seventh Congress," in Paul Finkelman and Donald R. Kennon, eds., *Civil War Congress and the Creation of Modern America* (Athens, Ohio, 2018), pp. 30–58.

[14] Joseph Reid, "Sharecropping in American History," in James Roumasset et al., eds., *Risk, Uncertainty, and Agricultural Development* (New York, 1979), pp. 283–319; Joseph Reid, "White Land, Black Labor and Agricultural Stagnation: The Causes and Effects of Sharecropping in the Postbellum South," *Explorations in Economic History* 16 (1979):31–55.

[15] Stephen DeCanio, "Accumulation and Discrimination in the Postbellum South," *Explorations in Economic History* 16 (1979):182–206; Robert Higgs, "Accumulation of Property by Southern Blacks before World War I," *American Economic Review* 72 (1982):725–37.

[16] For discussion, see Jenny Bourne (Wahl), "Give Lincoln Credit: How Paying for the Civil War Transformed the U.S. Financial System," *Albany Government Law Review* 3 (2010):700–39.

Fiat money essentially means that the government prints up pieces of paper and requires people—suppliers and soldiers—to accept them as legal tender. The Civil War–era federal government printed enormous amounts of the so-called greenbacks and other federal notes; not surprisingly, this led to substantial inflation. Despite the increased cost of living, the wages of white privates in the Union army remained constant until May 1864. Wages were even lower for black soldiers.[17]

The departure from specie was always intended to be temporary, and after the war the nation stumbled its way back to the prewar specie standard. Financial conservatives wanted to accomplish this quickly, but President Ulysses S. Grant allowed the reissuance of greenbacks to lubricate financial markets after the panic of 1873. The Senate under John Sherman (brother of William Tecumseh) subsequently drafted a resumption bill to return the United States to commodity money on January 1, 1879, and Grant signed it in January 1875.[18]

Because of population and productivity increases, the macroeconomy effectively "grew up" to the amount of currency in circulation. But considerable uncertainty remained about what the government might do and how much deflation to expect when.[19] Unanticipated price changes affect creditors and debtors differently, particularly when building flexibility into interest rates is difficult. In the nineteenth century (and much of the twentieth), fixed interest rates were nearly ubiquitous. Unexpected deflation thus hurt

---

[17]Wesley Mitchell, "Greenbacks and the Cost of the Civil War," *Journal of Political Economy* 5 (1897):139–67; U.S. National Archives, http://www.archives.gov/education/lessons/blacks-civil-war/.

[18]Jean Edward Smith, *Grant* (New York, 2001), pp. 578 ff.; William McFeeley, *Grant* (New York, 1981), p. 394.

[19]Because public officials wanted to resume specie payments at the exchange rate prevailing before the war and because Civil War inflation was massive, resumption required a revaluation of the currency and thus a decline in prices. James Kindahl, "Economic Factors in Specie Resumption in the United States, 1865–79," *Journal of Political Economy* 69 (1961):30–48; Irwin Unger, "The Business Community and the Origins of the 1875 Resumption Act," *Business History Review* 35 (1961):247–62; Richard Timberlake Jr., "Ideological Factors in Specie Resumption and Treasury Policy," *Journal of Economic History* 24 (1964):29–52; Jeffrey Williamson, "Watersheds and Turning Points: Conjectures on the Long-Term Impact of Civil War Financing," *Journal of Economic History* 34 (1974):636–61. One feature of the postbellum economy that made the transition back to commodity money easier was the rise of demand deposits, which meant that the number of bills in circulation was not as critical in determining the money supply. Charles Dunbar, "Deposits as Currency," *Quarterly Journal of Economics* 1 (1887):401–19.

46   *Jenny Bourne*

borrowers, who had to pay back in dollars that were worth more than when they were borrowed.

And who were the borrowers? Farmers, for one.

Particular Problems for Farmers

Not only did borrowing farmers suffer from unanticipated deflation, but farm prices fell faster than other prices during the immediate postbellum years. Farm income therefore did not keep up with the purchase prices for manufactured goods. After 1873, farm prices generally turned around, but they remained highly volatile, creating considerable uncertainty about expected farm revenue.[20]

What is more, although overall farm acreage grew, farm sizes shrank (fig. 4). This meant that people—particularly Southern blacks—had to farm their land more intensively than before.[21] As a consequence, agricultural productivity did not grow as fast as productivity in other sectors of the economy. Figure 5 shows that per capita real output was lower in the farm sector throughout the nineteenth century, with the gap widening significantly after the war.

Farmers were further frustrated by what some thought was price-gouging by railroads, particularly on short-haul routes where the local line held a monopoly. This frustration gave rise to the Granger movement, which unified farmers across the nation.[22] In fact, the first major postbellum national convention held in the South was a Granger gathering in Charleston, South Carolina, in 1875.[23] The aggregate macroeconomy did well after the war, but farmers understandably felt left behind.

---

[20] Morton Rothstein, "Farmer Movements and Organizations: Numbers, Gains, Losses," *Agricultural History* 62 (1988):161–81; Carter et al., *Historical Statistics*, Series Da1, Da14, Da28, Da1066; Bureau of Labor Statistics, U.S. Department of Labor, Consumer Price Index https://www.bls.gov/cpi/.

[21] Gavin Wright, *The Political Economy of the Cotton South* (New York, 1978), p. 181. Getting land into the hands of freed blacks was a major issue during Reconstruction, with most efforts being ineffective. Eric Foner, *Reconstruction, America's Unfinished Revolution 1873–1877* (New York, 1988), p. 375.

[22] Jenny Bourne, *In Essentials, Unity: An Economic History of the Grange Movement* (Athens, Ohio, 2017), offers an in-depth analysis of the Grangers.

[23] Solon Buck, *The Granger Movement: A Study of Agricultural Organization and Its Political, Economic, and Social Manifestations, 1870–1880* (1913; reprint ed., Lincoln, Neb., 1963), p. 279.

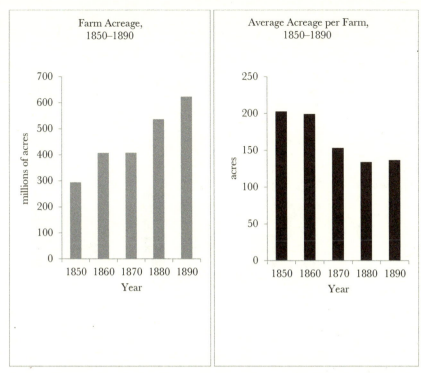

Fig. 4. Farm acreage and average farm size, 1850–90. Source: Gary Walton and Hugh Rockoff, *History of the American Economy* (Mason, Ohio, 2005), p. 287.

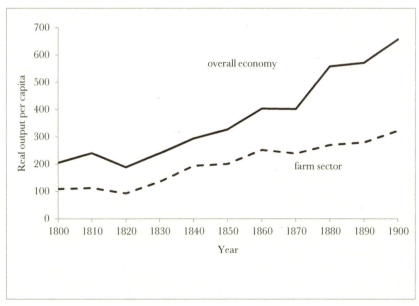

Fig. 5. Per capita real output, 1800–1900. Source: Carter et al., *Historical Statistics*, Series Ba817, Ca11, Da28, Da1285.

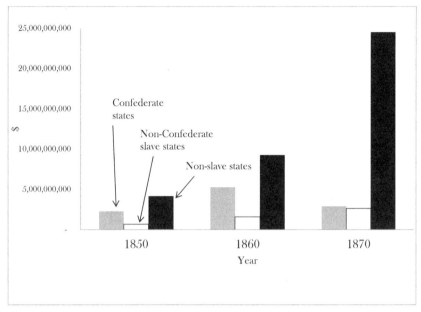

FIG. 6. Wealth by Region, 1850–70. Source: https://www2.census.gov/prod2/decennial/documents/1870c-01.pdf.

The South: A Wasteland

By far the largest postbellum discrepancy was regional. The North was larger than the South, both in geographic area and in population, so it is not surprising that the North also had more total wealth in 1850 than the South. But, as figure 6 shows, the difference grew much larger by 1870—in part because slaves no longer counted as wealth, and because much of the war's destruction took place on Southern soil. The South lost one-third of its hogs in the war, for instance.[24]

On a per person basis, output and income in the South compared favorably with that in the North on the eve of the Civil War. But real per capita output in the 1870s and 1880s in the South measured only half that in the North.[25]

---

[24] Wright, *Political Economy*, p. 164.
[25] The South received 26 percent of the nation's personal income in 1860 but only 15 percent by 1880. Per capita personal income in the South was 72 percent of the national

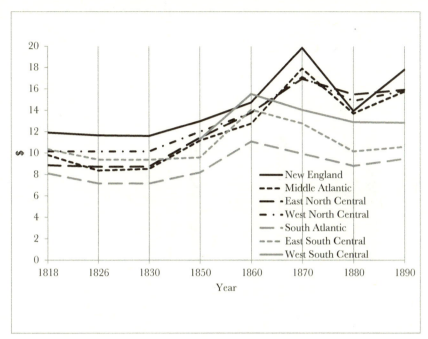

FIG. 7. Farm laborer monthly earnings with board by region, 1818–90. Source: Carter et al., *Historical Statistics*, Series Ba4234–43.

The cotton states stagnated even after the Reconstruction years. The annual growth rate in real per capita income between 1879 and 1899 in these states amounted to only half the rate for the United States as a whole.[26] Not only did the South have to adjust to a different sort of labor market after the war; it also had to cope with a large decline in world demand for cotton.[27]

Wages in the postbellum South lagged behind those in the North across economic sectors. Figure 7 shows that agricultural wages in the South Central region were roughly comparable to those in the North from 1818

---

average in 1860 but only 51 percent in 1880. Mark Aldrich, "Flexible Exchange Rates, Northern Expansion and the Market for Southern Cotton 1866–1879," *Journal of Economic History* 33 (1973):399–416; Foner, *Reconstruction*, p. 535.

[26]Roger Ransom and Richard Sutch, *One Kind of Freedom: The Economic Consequences of Emancipation* (New York, 1977), p. 192.

[27]Gavin Wright, "Cotton Competition and the Post-Bellum Recovery of the American South," *Journal of Economic History* 34 (1974):610–35; Wright, *Political Economy*, p. 181.

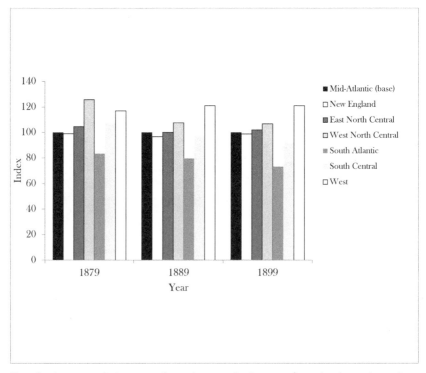

FIG. 8. Average relative annual earnings, males in manufacturing by region, 1879–99. Source: Joshua Rosenbloom, "Was There a National Labor Market at the End of the Nineteenth Century? New Evidence on Earnings in Manufacturing," *Journal of Economic History* 56 (1996):626–56.

until 1860; after the war, wages for farm labor were much higher in the North. Figure 8 reveals that manufacturing wages in the North and the West outstripped those in the South through the end of the nineteenth century.

Of course, the character of the regions was very different—the South was much more rural and much more devoted to agriculture, making its woes even more pronounced. During Reconstruction, the South generated only 11 percent of manufacturing despite containing more than a third of the population.[28] Inventive activity was practically nonexistent:

---

[28] Fred Bateman and Thomas Weiss, *A Deplorable Scarcity: The Failure of Industrialization in the Slave Economy* (Chapel Hill, N.C., 1981), p. 6.

Southerners held only 6.7 percent of new patents in 1880 and only 8 percent in 1910.[29]

Like Northern farmers, Southern ones often owed debts, so price deflation hit them hard. Obtaining currency and credit was even more difficult in the South than it was in the North. Adding to the South's misery was the advance of hookworm owing to unsanitary conditions spread by both armies. Hookworm affects physical stature as well as mental capacity, and over 40 percent of the postbellum Southern population suffered from it.[30] As one scholar put it, the South in the 1880s was very much like a third-world economy.[31]

Unsurprisingly, immigrants did not find the postbellum South attractive. About one-third of the native-born U.S. population lived in the South between 1865 and 1940, but less than 10 percent of the foreign-born.[32] And many of the more able or more fortunate Southerners simply packed up and moved out. According to census records, millions of people left the region bounded on the north by the Mason-Dixon Line and on the west by the Mississippi River in every decade between 1860 and 1890, even as population grew in other parts of the country.

Who stayed in the South? The poor and uneducated: those who could not afford to leave and those who had few prospects elsewhere. Lower wages in the South—especially for blacks—were due in part to the dismal state of schooling. In the cotton states in 1870, more than half of persons over age ten— and more than 90 percent of blacks age twenty and over—were illiterate.[33] After the war, Southern whites did not want to finance black education, and Southern employers did not want to lose workers to migration, so public schools generally languished.[34]

---

[29]Louis Ferleger, "Capital Goods and Southern Economic Development," *Journal of Economic History* 45 (1985):411–17.

[30]Garland Brinkley, "The Decline in Southern Agricultural Output, 1860–1880," *Journal of Economic History* 57 (1997):116–38.

[31]Edward Ayers, *The Promise of the New South: Life after Reconstruction* (New York, 1992), p. 22.

[32]Carter et al., *Historical Statistics*, Series Ad705–6; Joshua L. Rosenbloom, "Was There a National Labor Market at the End of the Nineteenth Century? New Evidence on Earnings in Manufacturing," *Journal of Economic History* 56 (1996):626–56.

[33]Roger Ransom and Richard Sutch, "Debt Peonage in the Cotton South after the Civil War," *Journal of Economic History* 32 (1972):641–69.

[34]Stephen DeCanio, "Agricultural Production, Supply, and Institutions in the Post-Civil War South," *Journal of Economic History* 32 (1972):396–98; Michelle Connolly, "Human Capital and Growth in the Postbellum South: A Separate but Unequal

52   *Jenny Bourne*

When the Redeemer governments returned in the 1880s, one of their first acts was to try to reduce public spending even more, as well as to implement regressive tax structures.[35] This made circumstances even worse for blacks and the poor. As of 1900, income for blacks was about 35 percent of white income in the United States as a whole, and the figure was even lower in the South.[36]

But leaving the South was not an option for many blacks, despite the dreadful conditions. Only after the huge reduction in foreign immigration to the United States around 1920—due mostly to restrictions enacted after World War I—did the great migration northward occur for black Americans.[37]

What Johnny Found

The postbellum U.S. economy was in some ways a golden age: economic growth was at an all-time high, and the nation was well on its way to becoming the world's largest economy. Amazingly, this took place on the heels of the most devastating war the country has ever known—a war in which one in four soldiers never returned home.

But the nation also suffered some ugly growing pains. Farmers did not share equally in productivity gains or wealth accumulation. Cities were rife with political corruption and xenophobia.[38] Industry created unsafe

---

Story," *Journal of Economic History* 64 (2004):363–99. Resentment ran rampant among Southern whites. Mississippi was on the verge of war in 1875, for instance, due to outrage over the black militia maintained by Governor Adelbert Ames. Franklin, *From Slavery*, p. 228.

[35]Ayers, *Promise of the New South*, p. 45.

[36]Robert Higgs, "Black Progress and the Persistence of Racial Economic Inequalities, 1865–1940," in William Darity and Steven Shulman, eds., *The Question of Discrimination: Racial Inequality in the U.S. Labor Market* (Middletown, Conn., 1989), pp. 9–31.

[37]William Collins, "When the Tide Turned: Immigration and the Delay of the Great Black Migration," *Journal of Economic History* 57 (1997):607–32; Connolly, "Human Capital."

[38]William Tweed of Tammany Hall is a prime example of political corruption. For a lively discussion, see Kenneth Anderson, *Boss Tweed* (New York, 2005). Likewise, the Chinese Exclusion Act of 1882 is one of the more egregious examples of postbellum xenophobia.

workplaces and horrible sorts of accidents, but existing law favored capital over labor.[39] And the South remained economically stunted for decades after the Civil War, with the brunt of misery falling on the poor and on former slaves.

---

[39]Attempts to regulate U.S. working conditions largely failed until the mid-1930s. The landmark case striking down workplace regulation is *Lochner v. New York*, 198 U.S. 45 (1905). Nineteenth-century free workers enjoyed much less legal protection than the owners of hired slaves; in fact, slave cases were used as precedent in postbellum cases to challenge mainstays of nineteenth-century employer defenses such as the fellow-servant rule and assumption-of-risk doctrine. Jenny Bourne (Wahl), *The Bondsman's Burden* (New York, 1998), chap. 3.

Anne Sarah Rubin

An Infamous Disregard?

Sherman's March and the Laws of War

MERCHANT OF TERROR." "Demon." "Attila." If you type "was
Sherman a . . ." into Google, the autocomplete includes "war crimi-
nal," "hero or villain," and with a few more letters "terrorist." The Urban
Dictionary, a popular website, describes General William Tecumseh
Sherman as having employed the "vicious" tactic of targeting civilians,
continuing:

> Such tactics had previously been deemed morally unacceptable. The delib-
> erate targeting of civilians for attack was taken up in World War II ending
> in the deaths of millions. The bombing of European cities by both sides of
> the war and Japanese cities by the U.S. as well as attacks on civilians
> in China, the Philippines, and Korea by Japan were consistent with and
> encouraged by Sherman's precedent. The logic of saving lives in the long-
> run by these tactics seems to have been refuted by history.

The "words related to General William T. Sherman" at the bottom of the
entry include *collateral damage, modern warfare, murder, terrorist,* and *war criminal.*[1] To be honest and fair, this is not the most reliable of sources. It is written by someone named "Tex in Tex," it misquotes the general, and the
word association also includes "war hero." But, it does represent a
popularly held view that William T. Sherman and the March through

[1] "General William T. Sherman," *The Urban Dictionary*, http://www.urbandictionary
.com, accessed Apr. 25, 2014.

54

Georgia and the Carolinas (figs. 1–4) during the final months of the Civil War have something to do with the creation of total war, and that the millions of civilian deaths in the wars of the twentieth and twenty-first centuries can be somehow laid at his feet.

Nor does this view reside entirely on the internet, noted repository of crackpot theories. A history of Henry County, Georgia, explains simply that "Sherman's March to the Sea was the first hint of the concept of 'Total War,' which was to come to full fruition during the Second World War, in which civilian infrastructure is considered a legitimate military target."[2] Later writers, notably James Reston Jr., tried to connect the March to atrocities in Vietnam, arguing that "when a rash Confederate ventured a shot on his trains from a courthouse, the courthouse was burned. When a lady burned her corncrib, she lost her house. The 'proportionality' of the retaliation is roughly the same, if geometrically less, as hostile fire from a jungle rifle being greeted by a B-52 strike."[3]

More recently, the writer Matthew Carr has used Sherman in a slightly more subtle fashion as the central figure in his "antimilitarist military history," *Sherman's Ghosts: Soldiers, Civilians, and the American Way of War*. While conceding the obvious point that there are vast differences between nineteenth and twenty-first-century warfare, Carr nevertheless argues that Sherman "embodies a very specific use of military force as an instrument of coercion and intimidation that has often been replayed by the U.S. Military and also by other armies."[4] In this case, the evils of mass warfare are not entirely Sherman's, but he still bears considerable responsibility, even if at times only symbolically.

Not that most writers even define what they mean by *total war* or *laws of war*. Often Sherman seems to be judged by the standards of today rather than those of his own time. Often *total war* seemed to refer to the degree of national mobilization, as opposed to the range of targets.[5] But a closer look

---

[2]Michael Reaves, *Historic Henry County* (San Antonio, Tex., 2004), p. 20.

[3]James Reston, *Sherman's March and Vietnam* (New York, 1984), pp. 92–93.

[4]Matthew Carr, *Sherman's Ghosts: Soldiers, Civilians, and the American Way of War* (New York, 2015), p. 8.

[5]Stig Förster and Jörg Nagler, eds., *On the Road to Total War: The American Civil War and German Wars of Unification, 1861–1871* (Cambridge, 1997), p. 8. Mark A. Smith has argued that Sherman did not stray far from the teachings of Jomini and Clausewitz on the March. Mark A. Smith, "Sherman's Unexpected Companions: Marching through Georgia with Jomini and Clausewitz," *Georgia Historical Quarterly* 81 (1997):1–24. Several historians have

FIG. 1. "Sherman's March to the Sea," by Felix Octavius Carr Darley, engraved by Alexander Hay Ritchie, ca. 1868. *(Library of Congress Prints and Photographs Division)*

FIG. 2. "Contrabands accompanying the line of Sherman's march through Georgia," *Frank Leslie's Illustrated Newspaper*, Mar. 18, 1865. *(Library of Congress Prints and Photographs Division)*

FIG. 3. Regiment of Michigan engineers and mechanics destroying railroad tracks in Atlanta, from a stereograph by George N. Barnard. *(Library of Congress Prints and Photographs Division)*

FIG. 4. "Sherman's March through South Carolina—Burning of McPhersonville, February 5, 1865," *Harper's Weekly*, Mar. 4, 1865. *(Library of Congress Prints and Photographs Division)*

58   *Anne Sarah Rubin*

at Sherman's March, in the context of the changing nature of Union policies over the course of the war, paints a more nuanced picture.

The Laws of Hard War

In 1864 there were no Hague or Geneva conventions to govern the actions of belligerents. That is not to say there were no guides for military behavior and conduct. But those rules were also fluid and evolving, changing as the very nature of the Civil War changed. Initial Union policy toward the nascent Confederacy and its civilians had been one of conciliation. Essentially, it was designed to animate a perceived silent majority of Unionists, and it emphasized the targeting of armies rather than civilians. In effect, Southern civilians were still treated as American citizens rather than as belligerents.

But as early as 1862 that had begun to change. During the summer of 1862, Union General John Pope issued a series of orders that allowed the Army of Virginia to subsist on the produce of the local countryside (among other things), and a desperately frustrated Lincoln approved them. Pope's soldiers went on a tear of destruction and violence reminiscent of the stories that would come out of Georgia and the Carolinas two years later. So great were the abuses perpetrated on civilians that Pope was forced to condemn his own men.[6]

Once Lincoln issued the preliminary Emancipation Proclamation in September 1862, the opportunity for conciliation was over and the war would become, in Mark Grimsley's phrase, "hard-handed." At the same time, Union General in Chief Henry Halleck had been consulting with the Prussian-born professor Francis Lieber about devising a military code. Lieber had already drafted two more limited opinions—one dealing with

---

explored the question of whether Sherman's March qualified as "total war": Mark Grimsley, "Modern War/Total War," in Steven E. Woodworth, ed., *The American Civil War: A Handbook of Literature and Research* (Westport, Conn., 1996), pp. 379–89; Mark A. Neely Jr., "Was the Civil War a Total War?," *Civil War History* 50 (2004):434–58; Wayne Wei-Siang Hsieh, "Total War and the American Civil War Reconsidered: The End of an Outdated 'Master Narrative,'" *Journal of the Civil War Era* 1 (2011):394.

[6]Daniel Sutherland, "Abraham Lincoln, John Pope, and the Origins of Total War," *Journal of Military History* 56 (1992):577, 580, 584.

the treatment of captured Confederate soldiers, and the other, more significant one with Confederate guerrillas and other partisans.[7] Lieber called his
1863 comprehensive work *A Code for the Government of Armies*, but the War
Department issued it as General Orders No. 100 and it is popularly known
as the Lieber Code.[8] The code was designed to codify the laws of war, especially as they pertained to interactions between civilians and soldiers.

One of the most significant sections of the code was its relatively broad
construction of "military necessity." In the language of Article 15:

> Military necessity admits of all direct destruction of life or limb of armed
> enemies, and of other persons whose destruction is incidentally unavoidable
> in the armed contests of the war; it allows of the capturing of every armed
> enemy, and every enemy of importance to the hostile government, or of pecu-
> liar danger to the captor; it allows of all destruction of property, and obstruc-
> tion of the ways and channels of traffic, travel, or communication, and of all
> withholding of sustenance or means of life from the enemy; of the appropria-
> tion of whatever an enemy's country affords necessary for the subsistence
> and safety of the army, and of such deception as does not involve the breaking
> of good faith either positively pledged, regarding agreements entered into
> during the war, or supposed by the modern law of war to exist. Men who
> take up arms against one another in public war do not cease on this account
> to be moral beings, responsible to one another and to God.

Lieber's relatively broad definition, while deploring "cruelty" and acts of
vengeance, did allow the making of war on civilians in certain manners and
circumstances. For example, Article 17 explicitly permitted using starvation
of civilians as a method of putting pressure on an enemy. This was because,
according to the code, a citizen of a hostile nation or enemy was "one of
the constituents of the hostile state or nation, and as such is subjected to the

---

[7]The latter pamphlet, *Guerrilla Parties Considered with Reference to the Laws and Usages of
War*, was drafted in 1862 at the request of General Halleck. Its conclusions were largely
incorporated into the full Lieber Code. Paul Finkelman, "Francis Lieber and the Modern
Law of War," review of *Lincoln's Code: The Laws of War in American History*, by John Fabian
Witt, *University of Chicago Law Review* 80, no. 4 (Fall 2013):2071–132, 2084–86; Stephen C.
Neff, *Justice in Blue and Gray: A Legal History of the Civil War* (Cambridge, Mass., 2010),
pp. 76–77; John Fabian Witt, *Lincoln's Code: The Laws of War in American History* (New York,
2012), pp. 193–94.

[8]David Bosco, "Moral Principle vs. Military Necessity," *The American Scholar*, 2008;
Burrus M. Carnahan, "Lincoln, Lieber, and the Laws of War: The Origins and Limits of
the Principle of Military Necessity," *American Journal of International Law* 92 (1998):213–31.

hardships of the war."[9] The other factor to keep in mind about the code is that it was designed in part to justify short, sharp wars. The more intense and punishing a war, Lieber believed, the sooner it would be over. In a sense, the code enshrined an idea of war as, perhaps paradoxically, both ferocious and humanitarian.[10]

Among the code's prohibitions, however, was the theft and/or destruction of artworks and the like (Article 35); and, under the punishment of death, "all wanton violence committed against persons in the invaded country, all destruction of property not commanded by the authorized officer, all robbery, all pillage or sacking, even after taking a place by main force, all rape, wounding, maiming, or killing of such inhabitants."[11]

Confederates claimed that the code was so broad as to license "mischief" under the grounds of military necessity; certainly, by 1864 Lincoln and the Union had become comfortable with a high degree of destruction of private property (cotton and the contents of homes, if not homes themselves) in areas such as Missouri and the Shenandoah Valley.[12] Thus one could argue that the Lieber Code, at least as it pertained to the treatment of civilians, was honored more in the breach than closely followed.[13]

Francis J. Lippitt's *Field Service in War*, a manual on military logistics published just after the war, leans on military necessity to justify foraging, arguing that it was a "well-established right of war." But at the same time, Lippitt did concede that it was incumbent on commanders and soldiers to restrain themselves. To do otherwise would be to bring dishonor on the country.[14] Lippitt's own work demonstrates the complexity of the moral issues surrounding foraging. By its very nature, the act of seizing supplies inflicts hardships on the civilian population. To inflict the least amount of harm (and thus to operate within the moral, if not the legal, boundaries of so-called civilized warfare), tight control must be maintained. Without

---

[9]"General Orders No. 100: The Lieber Code," http://avalon.law.yale.edu/19th _century/lieber.asp.

[10]Finkelman, "Francis Lieber and the Modern Law of War," pp. 2101–2.

[11]"General Orders No. 100: The Lieber Code," Article 44, http://avalon.law.yale.edu /19th_century/lieber.asp#sec2.

[12]Carnahan, "Lincoln, Lieber, and the Laws of War," pp. 218, 228.

[13]Bosco, "Moral Principle vs. Military Necessity."

[14]Francis J. Lippitt, *Field Service in War: Comprising Marches, Convoys, Camps and Cantonments, Reconnaissances, Outposts, Foraging, and Notes on Logistics* (New York, 1869), pp. 115–18.

defined foraging parties and a centralized distribution system—that is, when a commander allowed troops to supply themselves—chaos would ensue. Specifically, Lippitt warned, it would lead:

(1) To an entire relaxation of discipline without which a military force is only an armed mob.

(2) To universal pillage, and to murders and other outrages by the troops upon the inhabitants, which always follow in its train.

(3) To the consequent massacre of straggling parties, in retaliation, by the inhabitants, who are thus made bitter enemies.

(4) To an enormous waste and destruction of the supplies themselves over and above what is actually consumed.[15]

One might have expected Lippitt to use the recent example of Sherman's March, but he did not, hearkening instead to Napoleon's Russian campaign.

Lippitt did not just ignore the March; he defended it, noting Sherman's orders that when seizing household goods the men carefully "discriminat[ed] between the rich, who were generally hostile to us, and the poor and industrious, who were usually friendly or at least neutral." Also, he described an organized and controlled system, complete with detailed rules and receipts. Any deviations from the prescribed system were the fault of a few bad apples, stragglers, and the like, not the main force of marchers.[16]

Sherman's Laws

Despite innumerable allegations to the contrary, Sherman himself was well aware that war was governed by rules, and must have been familiar with the Lieber Code. In fact, Sherman's aide Major Henry Hitchcock was the nephew of one of Lieber's collaborators and maintained a correspondence with Lieber throughout the March.[17] Sherman's knowledge allowed him to shape his orders and campaign such that they skated just up to the edge of legality as he understood it. This is best seen in two examples: Sherman's

---

[15]Ibid., pp. 130, 135.
[16]Ibid., pp. 138–39.
[17]Witt, *Lincoln's Code*, p. 280.

62 Anne Sarah Rubin

expulsion of civilians from Atlanta in September 1864, and then the March itself, taken as a whole.

Sherman's army took control of the city of Atlanta on September 2, 1864. Sherman had no plans to remain there for the long term; rather, he sought to turn the city into a purely military base, a place for his soldiers to briefly rest and resupply. He did not want to have to worry about either caring for civilians or protecting his men from spies and guerrilla actions. To that end, on September 4 he issued Special Field Orders No. 67, which began quite simply, stating: "The city of Atlanta, being exclusively required for warlike purposes, will at once be vacated by all except the armies of the United States and such civilian employees as may be retained by the proper departments of the government." Over the following days, additional orders directed civilians to register and then make arrangements to be moved through the lines either north or south of the city.[18]

Those who would condemn Sherman for making unjustified war on noncombatants have often pointed to this incident as a prime example. One reason may be the series of increasingly angry correspondence between Sherman and Confederate General John Bell Hood and Atlanta's mayor James M. Calhoun between September 7 and September 14. These letters, in which Hood and Calhoun argue with Sherman about the expulsion, show us Sherman at his most controlled and analytical.[19]

The first letter is from Sherman to Hood on September 7, asking for Hood's assistance in evacuating civilians toward the south, via the town of Rough and Ready. Hood replied on September 9, agreeing to appoint guards to assist in the process, but then he continued: "And now, sir, permit me to say that the unprecedented measure you propose transcends, in studied and ingenious cruelty, all acts ever before brought to my attention in the dark history of war."[20] Sherman countered this charge by pointing out that Hood himself used and destroyed civilian homes during the defense of Atlanta. Sherman then went on to remind Hood that it was Southerners who in fact

---

[18]Stephen Davis, *What the Yankees Did to Us: Sherman's Bombardment and Wrecking of Atlanta* (Macon, Ga., 2012), pp. 290–95; Wendy Hammond Venet, *A Changing Wind: Commerce and Conflict in Civil War Atlanta* (New Haven, Conn., 2014), pp. 174–77; Special Field Orders 67, in *The War of the Rebellion: A Compilation of the Official Records of the Union and Confederate Armies* (Washington, D.C., 1880–1901), ser. 1, vol. 38, part 5, p. 837 (hereafter *O.R.*).

[19]For an extremely detailed discussion, see Davis, *What the Yankees Did to Us*, pp. 297–308. The entire correspondence can be found in *O.R.*, ser. 1, vol. 39, part 2, pp. 414–22.

[20]*O.R.*, ser. 1, vol. 39, part 2, p. 415.

An Infamous Disregard? 63

plunged the nation into war. Sherman argued that his removal of women and children from the zone of battle was in fact "a kindness" and "more humane" than leaving them in place, subject to battle and attack.[21] Sherman therefore staked out the position that by forcing civilians out of Atlanta, he was in fact protecting rather than attacking them.

Hood would have none of that. He charged Sherman with violating the customs "usual in war among civilized nations" by shelling Atlanta without warning. Hood then went on to challenge Sherman's complaints about the Confederacy as a whole, closing with a final denial of Sherman's legitimacy.[22] Sherman then responded testily, "I was not bound by the laws of war to give notice of the shelling of Atlanta, a 'fortified town' with magazines, arsenals, foundries, and public stores. You were bound to take notice. See the books."[23] Sherman could hardly have been more explicit than this in his demonstration that he believed himself to be working within the rules of legitimate warfare.

But this is not the most quoted passage from the September exchanges of letters. Rather, those who would condemn Sherman often point to his September 12, 1864, letter to the mayor and city council of Atlanta, in which Sherman wrote that "war is cruelty and you cannot refine it," to make the argument that he was willing to do whatever worked to wreak all kinds of havoc on civilians in order to end the war. But to quote only that line is to miss the fuller context of his reply. Sherman's letter went on to make the point that his ultimate goal was peace, and that only a speedy end to the war would bring that about. A harsher war, Sherman believed, would be a shorter one. Or, as he explained, "I want peace, and believe it can now only be reached through union and war, and I will ever conduct war with a view to perfect an early success." Then Sherman went on, "but, my dear sirs, when that peace does come, you may call on me for anything. Then will I share with you the last cracker, and watch with you to shield your homes and families against danger from every quarter." Hard war was not vindictive or punitive, Sherman believed, but a means to an end. Once the war was over, so too would be the harshness.[24] In making this claim, Sherman

---

[21] Ibid., p. 416.
[22] Ibid., pp. 419–22.
[23] Ibid., p. 422.
[24] Ibid., p. 419.

demonstrated that he was in fact operating within the boundaries of a code that allowed war to be made on civilians.[25]

What of the March itself? Before leaving Atlanta on November 15, 1864, Sherman set some ground rules for his 62,000 men. He did this in the form of his Special Field Orders No. 120. The nine articles described the divisions of his army, their marching orders, and, importantly for our purposes, what the army could and could not do. The men were instructed to "forage liberally on the country" and "to destroy mills, houses, cotton-gins, etc," but within limits. The foraging parties were supposed to be regularized and under the control of "discreet" officers; soldiers were not supposed to enter homes; should the army be left "unmolested," Southern property was also supposed to be left alone. Significantly, Sherman also ordered that when seizing livestock, his men ought to discriminate "between the rich, who are usually hostile, and the poor and industrious, usually neutral or friendly." If the army was well treated, they were instructed to "leave with each family a reasonable portion for their maintenance."[26]

As for African Americans, Sherman was willing to permit commanders to put "able-bodied" men who could "be of service" into pioneer corps, but urged them to be mindful of their limited supplies. Well aware of his logistical limitations, Sherman wanted his officers to leave the newly freed women and children behind.[27]

Most of these rules were honored more in the breach than in reality, but their very existence gave Sherman (and to an arguably lesser extent his men) a degree of moral cover. They undoubtedly allowed for a certain elasticity— harsher treatment of some people in some places, leniency elsewhere. The problem with them seemed to arise from the degree to which individual Union soldiers were left to their own discretion when foraging. In that way real damage and devastation, arguably beyond the boundaries of what was intended by the code, did happen. But it is important to remember that the worst destruction seems to have happened in violation of orders, rather than in service of them.[28]

---

[25]Witt, *Lincoln's Code*, p. 252.

[26]Special Field Orders 120, *O.R.*, ser. 1, vol. 39, pp. 713–14.

[27]*O.R.*, ser. 1, vol. 39, part 3, pp. 713–14; William T. Sherman, *Memoirs of General William T. Sherman* (Bloomington, Ind., 1957), pp. 175–76.

[28]Witt, *Lincoln's Code*, pp. 281–82; Finkelman, "Francis Lieber and the Modern Law of War," pp. 2102, 2105; Carr, *Sherman's Ghosts*, p. 116.

Sherman believed he was operating within the laws of war and parameters of so-called civilized behavior, but that did not mean that he was unwilling to push up against the boundaries of those rules. Frightening people, stealing their supplies, even burning their barns was one thing; wholesale killing or raping, as happened in areas riven by guerrilla violence, was beyond the pale. One could argue that Sherman exploited the language of violence and fear in order to reach his ends. Sherman biographer Michael Fellman has argued that while the March "stopped well short of a 'total war' in the twentieth century Nazi sense," Sherman's rhetoric of destruction implied that he could make war on whomever he chose, and that Southern whites would be powerless to stop him.[29]

Did that make Sherman a terrorist? He certainly used calculated brutality to terrorize the Southern population. Fellman describes Sherman as having "terrorist capacities."[30] And what responsibility, for both destroying and reigning themselves in, accrues to the soldiers on the March? Part of the reason that the March was not *total* in the twentieth-century sense was because the soldiers limited themselves, held back by their own internal, cultural sense of morality.[31]

Sherman himself may have overstepped the bounds of legality a few times, each time in retaliation for Confederate actions, each time regarding his use of prisoners of war. In the first instance, when Sherman learned of torpedoes or mines buried outside Savannah, he called for prisoners to be brought up to clear them. In the second, when Union foragers were captured and killed by Wade Hampton's men in South Carolina, Sherman ordered prisoners to draw lots and chose one to be killed, thus setting an example.[32]

But what keeps Sherman from being a terrorist, in the modern sense of the word, is that he was operating during wartime, with the full sanction and support of his government. When the war ended, so too did his hostilities and destruction. A better analogy to terrorism in the wake of the

---

[29]Michael Fellman, *Citizen Sherman: A Life of William Tecumseh Sherman* (New York, 1995), pp. 171, 179; Michael Fellman, "At the Nihilist Edge: Reflections on Guerrilla Warfare during the American Civil War," in Förster and Nagler, *On the Road to Total War*, p. 535.

[30]Fellman, *Citizen Sherman*, pp. 182–83.

[31]Ibid., pp. 225–26.

[32]Cornelius Cadle, "An Adjutant's Recollections," in *Sketches of War History, 1861–1865*, Papers read before the Ohio Commandry of the Military Order of the Loyal Legion of the United States, 9 vols. (Cincinnati, Ohio, 1883–93), 5:397–99.

66   *Anne Sarah Rubin*

Civil War would be the waves of violence that confronted African Americans during Reconstruction as they sought to exercise their new economic, social, and political freedoms.

The notion that Sherman brought forth a different kind of war with the March makes sense only retrospectively. As the nineteenth century became the twentieth, and as wars of increasing deadliness and destructive power broke out around the globe, the March seemed to reappear again and again. Often, the analogy was strained, but it revealed much about the common understanding of the March, or of a simplified version of it.

Modern War

In 1902 a humor column in the *New York Times* reproached the Democrats for criticizing soldiers' activities in the Philippines. Written by Robert Welch in the colloquial voice of Silas Larrabee of Ogunquit, Maine, the column called for loyalty to the soldiers (rather than criticism). He minimized the cruelties perpetuated on the Filipinos, comparing them first to American activities against Indians in the West, and then moved on to the more distant past:

> And how about Sherman's march through Georgy? That was deverstation, wasn't it? And didn't the people of the North say it was a good job? Ever know a band up North that couldn't play 'Marchin' Through Georgy? Why they sing it to babies—make it a cradle song. Somehow I rayther think when we come to know the hull story we'll pootty much all of us agree that Smith's operations was jest about on a level with Sherman's accordin' to.[33]

Welch highlighted an essential hypocrisy: if Americans were comfortable with swaths of destruction at home, why should they have a problem with them further afield? If excuses could be made for Sherman's bummers, why not for Gen. Jacob H. Smith's soldiers? In fact, this was part of the very defense offered before Senator Henry Cabot Lodge's committee investigating American conduct during the so-called Philippine Insurrection, which resulted in the deaths of several hundred thousand Filipino civilians.[34]

---

[33]"Mr. Larrabee Defends the Army," *New York Times*, May 11, 1902.
[34]Carr, *Sherman's Ghosts*, pp. 152–58.

Over a decade later, Sherman's March reappeared in the national and international discourse, as Germany marched through Belgium, and the world erupted into war. A piece in the *New York Times* in September 1914 attempted to calculate the collective cost of all wars in human history, concluding that the human toll was some fifteen billion lives. As for the cost of destroyed property, the authors threw up their metaphorical hands, determining it to be both "enormous" and incalculable. This is where Sherman's March came in: they used it as an example, citing Sherman's own estimate of $300 million in property destroyed. But the value of the property lost in the Civil War would pale in comparison to the amount currently at risk in Europe, particularly in Belgium and France. In this instance, the devastation of Sherman's March is being minimized rather than connected to the wars of the twentieth century.[35]

More commonly, the devastation of Sherman's March was used to remind Americans of the costs of war, however justifiable. William M. Sloane of Columbia University prophetically called the war "a world disaster of unparalleled significance" and warned against American intervention overseas. He cautioned Americans against becoming too outraged by atrocities perpetrated against civilians, lest that lead them to intervene. Patronizingly, Sloane opined that "the sense of outrage which Americans feel over the horrors of war, while most creditable to them, is very often based upon an ignorance of the rules and regulations of so-called civilized warfare, and upon a sentimentality which, though also very creditable, is unfortunately not one of the factors in the world's work." He called on his readers to put their sentimentality aside and to recall both Sherman's March and Hunter's 1864 Valley Campaign, noting "and yet at that time, in what we considered the supreme danger to our country, the conduct of those men was approved and they themselves were almost deified for their actions."[36] Sloane seems to be saying to readers that if Sherman could be not only forgiven but also celebrated, then Americans should also remember the Monroe Doctrine and give the Germans a pass in the interests of their own security.

---

[35]"Fifteen Billion Human Lives Have Been Sacrificed in War since the Beginning of Authentic History," *New York Times*, Sept. 13, 1914.

[36]"Prof. Sloane Warns America against War," *New York Times*, Sept. 20, 1914.

68   *Anne Sarah Rubin*

These early references to the Civil War and Sherman continued to pop up during the years of World War I. In May 1915, Yandell Henderson of Yale University wrote a pro-German column in the *New York Times*, again encouraging American neutrality. Henderson minimized Germany's invasion of Belgium, and then went on:

> as for atrocities, Belgium, Serbia, East Prussia, and Poland have probably been no more thoroughly desolated than Georgia after Sherman's march to the Sea. Away from ordinary social restraints, men always do such things. It is rare for a militia company here to have a field day, or a college class to hold a reunion without a certain percentage making beasts of themselves.

Like earlier writers, Henderson downplayed the March in order to make his broader political point: atrocities overseas should not warrant intervention, and America should not go to war with Germany.[37]

Henderson's letter prompted a series of angry responses. The historian G. M. Trevelyan listed the atrocities being perpetrated in Europe, and challenged Henderson's "boys will be boys" attitude. The attacks on civilians in Europe did not constitute normal behavior by soldiers or young men, and Trevelyan wrote to "deny that Sherman's troops either burned women and children alive or gouged peoples eyes out or murdered civilians wholesale, as the Austro-Hungarian troops did in Serbia."[38] The following day's paper contained a letter from Mary Cadwalader Jones, who had lived in the South during the waning days of the Civil War. She remembered seeing "grim" evidence of devastation and starving civilians, "but here were no 'atrocities' and no 'frightfulness.'" She deplored the damage, for which she blamed bummers and faithless slaves, "but it was not accompanied by beastliness or cruelty, nor was the desolation to be even compared with that of Belgium and Serbia now."[39] This flies in the face of the conventional wisdom that to Southern whites Sherman's March was the ultimate destruction, the worst of the worst.

George Haven Putnam, whose Civil War career included service in New Orleans in 1862, the Shenandoah Valley in 1864, and North Carolina and Savannah in 1865, joined the attack against Yandell Henderson. Henderson drew a distinction between Germany's officially ordered and sanctioned

---

[37]Yandell Henderson, "Ourselves as Germans See Us," *New York Times*, May 21, 1915.
[38]G. M. Trevelyan, "An Historian Mystified," *New York Times*, May 22, 1915.
[39]Mary Cadwalader Jones, "What Sherman's Men Did," *New York Times*, May 26, 1915.

shootings of civilians, sinking of ships, and generally making war on non-combatants and the destruction of property in the Civil War South. Putnam perceived Henderson's essay as an attack on the honor and reputation of American (read Union) soldiers, and one that he felt was not befitting a professor at Yale.[40]

Thus far the responses to Henderson's initial article took issue with his equating Sherman's March and German attacks on civilians. But at least one reader, a military historian named John A. Bigelow, thought that the quest to minimize Civil War antecedents went too far. Bigelow rightly pointed out that just because Sherman's men were not as brutal as German troops does not mean that they should be absolved of all guilt. Bigelow noted that the men of 1864 and 1865 went well beyond their written orders and seemed to be unstoppable. Is "an army which waits to act frightfully, until it is ordered to do so . . . more to be criticized than one which resorts to such action without orders and persists in it when ordered to desist?" wondered Bigelow. That is, where do the moral bearings of the men themselves come in? Isn't terrorizing civilians terrorizing civilians, whether under orders or not? Similarly, Putnam wondered, "If Sherman was not wanton in his harshness because he had a military object in it, may not the Germans be similarly justified?" Bigelow raised one of the central moral questions of the March and its legacy: do we retrospectively excuse the excesses of Sherman's men because we agree with their cause? Do we excuse them because they won?[41]

In an editorial on June 15, the editors of the *New York Times* weighed in on the controversy, proclaiming that "Georgia was not Belgium." They reminded their readers that the "atrocities" in Belgium shocking the world included using civilians as shields, misuse of white flags, taking and murdering hostages—all crimes of which Sherman's men were not even accused, much less guilty.[42] The next column featured a reply to Bigelow, this one advocating intervention precisely because of the level of German cruelty against civilians, which was so much greater than that of the Union army.[43]

---

[40]George Haven Putnam, "War as We Made It," *New York Times*, June 4, 1915.

[41]John A. Bigelow, "Nothing but Their Eyes to Weep With," *New York Times*, June 13, 1915. Bigelow is the author of *The Principles of Strategy* (Philadelphia, 1894). Bigelow's letter was also reprinted as "Did Grant, Sherman and Sheridan Teach Militarism to Germany?," *William and Mary College Quarterly Historical Magazine* 24 (July 1915):66–72.

[42]"Georgia Was Not Belgium," *New York Times*, June 15, 1915.

[43]Frank Jewett Mather Jr., "The Degree of War," *New York Times*, June 15, 1915.

70   *Anne Sarah Rubin*

Bigelow responded in turn on June 19, arguing that the differences in execution between the Germans and Sherman's men did not account for similarities in impulse. That is, both sides were animated by the same intentions: "Each officer placed efficiency before humanity, except so far as efficiency meant humanity to him. If one may take Sherman at his word, he would not have stopped at a massacre had it seemed to him necessary to the attainment of his military object." Bigelow went on to clarify his earlier point about the differences between 1864–65 and 1914–15, explaining that "things do not have to be parallel to be properly comparable." Bigelow continued to insist on the utility of the American past for the global present.[44]

Once the United States became involved in World War I, the usable past of Sherman's March ceased to be a significant point of discussion.[45] The analogy reappeared briefly after the war, during testimony before the Senate Committee on Propaganda in 1919. Grant Squires, a New York lawyer who visited Belgium, testified to the cruelties he saw perpetrated by the Germans: men and women beaten with rifle butts, children and babies murdered, and families starving without shelter. Squires was then asked to counter earlier testimony by German sympathizer Edmund von Mach, to the effect that Sherman's March had "also been a very cruel expedition." This enraged Senator Knute Nelson (a Civil War veteran), who angrily proclaimed that American soldiers had never "killed women and children. Whatever they did, they did not do that." Nelson specifically asked Squires to address von Mach's charges that the Germans were no worse than Sherman's men; Squires confirmed that the Germans were different from any predecessors.[46]

Essentially, what this exchange shows is that a new standard was being set for violations of civilians. Where once the thefts and fires of Sherman's men were the worst that could be imagined, the Great War issued horrors of an entirely different order of magnitude.

Not everyone got the memo that Sherman was no longer the epitome of evil. The English novelist, critic, and travel writer Ford Madox Ford reflected

---

[44] John Bigelow, "Georgia and Belgium," *New York Times,* June 19, 1915.

[45] Some contributors to *Confederate Veteran* complained about this new silence. See Henry E. Shepherd, "Historic Ironies—Sherman and German," *Confederate Veteran* 26 (Jan. 1918):17–19; Will T. Hale, "Historic Exposures Commended," *Confederate Veteran* 26 (Feb. 1918):91.

[46] "Tells of German Insurance Scheme," *New York Times,* Jan. 10, 1916; "Tells of Horrors Seen in Belgium," *New York Times,* Jan. 16, 1919.

on Sherman during his travels in the United States during the 1930s. Unlike other writers who began their musings by visiting the sites of the March (whether in Georgia or the Carolinas), Ford began his reverie far away, at the home where a woman was killed during the Battle of Gettysburg. Why was such a fuss made over this one unfortunate woman, he wondered, as "there were plenty women killed and worse by Sherman's licensed plunderers, and one does not much bother about them."[47] Ford then went on to condemn Sherman for burning "Columbus" (clearly he meant Columbia), blaming Wade Hampton, and admitting that his soldiers were drunk when they did it. He compared the burning of Columbia to the burning of Liège, Belgium, but noted approvingly that "the Great German Staff had at least the decency to deny fiercely that their troops were drunk," regardless of whether they were actually inebriated or not. Ford praised Confederate generals Robert E. Lee and Stonewall Jackson while condemning Grant, Sherman, and Sheridan as "murderers" who disobeyed "the dictates of humanity." His ultimate point, clearly influenced as much by his World War I experiences as his travels in America, is that

> it is silly to say that the butchering of civilians shortens wars and is therefore more humane. . . . Or burning their houses or crops or furniture or clothing. I suppose that if you completely wiped out a whole nation, civilians plus armed forces, you might stop a war. But, horrible as they are, modern methods of war are not as efficient as all that—and not quite stamped out peoples develop a philoprogenitiveness, a tenacity of purpose, a vindictiveness.[48]

The "war to end all wars" reanimated debates over attacks on civilians. Ford was certainly right about the vindictiveness that would continue to burn through the survivors of scorched-earth tactics.

There were few mentions of Sherman's March during World War II, but the Vietnam War, perhaps because it coincided with the centennial of the Civil War, raised more analogies to it. The historian Theodore Rosengarten recalled being astonished in the 1960s and 1970s when he heard a variety of cultural critics and opponents of the war in Vietnam (including Mary McCarthy, Howard Levine, and Michael Hess) "compare Sherman's operations in Georgia and the Carolinas to crimes committed by Americans in Vietnam. They called Sherman our first merchant of terror, the spiritual

---

[47]Ford Madox Ford, *Great Trade Route* (New York, 1937), p. 243.
[48]Ibid., 299; Hale, "Historic Exposures Commended," p. 302.

72   *Anne Sarah Rubin*

father of such hated doctrines as search and destroy, pacification, strategic hamlets, free-fire zones. You had to wonder whether without Sherman the atom bomb might not have been dropped."[49] Perhaps the connection had to do with loss and defeat, as C. Vann Woodward described in *The Burden of Southern History*. Perhaps it had to do with the intimacy of the fighting and the hand-to-hand targeting of civilians, different from the massive battles of World War II. Perhaps it had to do with the need to knit a divided nation back together.

The most detailed and culturally significant exploration of this relationship came in James Reston Jr.'s 1984 book, *Sherman's March and Vietnam*. Reston retraced the March through Georgia, looking to the past to explain the more turbulent present. He seemed at times to draw a straight line of connection between nineteenth- and twentieth-century violence:

> Gen. William Tecumseh Sherman is considered by many to be the author of "total war," the first general of modern human history to carry the logic of war to its ultimate extreme, the first to scorch the earth, the first to wreck an economy in order to starve its soldiers. He was our first "merchant of terror," and the spiritual father, some contend, of our Vietnam concepts of "search and destroy," "pacification," "strategic hamlets," "free fire zones." As such he remains a cardboard figure of our history: a monstrous archvillain to unreconstructed Southerners, an embarrassment to Northerners who wonder if "civilized war" died with him, whether without Sherman the atom bomb might not have been dropped or Vietnam entered.[50]

Reston did concede that the connection was more metaphorical than real, but at the same time he raised real questions about limits during wartime, and how those limits could shift. What was the conceptual or theoretical difference between destroying property and killing people?

While conceding that much of what Americans thought about Sherman (and by extension his men) was informed by mythology rather than facts, those myths mattered. Reston wanted to shape the inevitable mythologizing of the Vietnam experience as well. Thus, he concluded that "Sherman's soldiers and Westmoreland's soldiers have important things in common."[51]

---

[49]Theodore Rosengarten, "New Views on the Burning of Columbia," in *University South Caroliniana Society: Fifty Sixth Annual Meeting*, 1993.
[50]Reston, *Sherman's March and Vietnam*, p. 6.
[51]Ibid., pp. 7–8.

What they had in common, Reston argued, was being animated by a desire for vengeance and reprisals. Where they differed was in questions of scale, which was as much a function of technology as of desire.[52] Men in the twentieth century had weapons of mass destruction; Union soldiers did not.

What of today? Sherman is sometimes invoked in discussions of the Iraq War, often in support of a more terrible or total sort of war. On April 28, 2014, my trusty Google Alert pointed me to a column by Thomas Ricks in *Foreign Policy*. Entitled "Sherman as a Counterinsurgent," Ricks's article argues that Sherman carried out not a soft "hearts and minds" campaign but a "tough-minded" "you're either with us or against us" approach, with clear political and psychological dimensions.[53] I am not convinced by his argument, but I am convinced that Sherman's March, and its relationship to what Americans think about war, is still very much alive and relevant today.

---

[52]Ibid., pp. 15–16.
[53]Thomas E. Ricks, "Sherman as a Counterinsurgent," *Foreign Policy*, Apr. 28, 2014, http://ricks.foreignpolicy.com/posts/2014/04/28/sherman_as_a_counterinsurgent.

Paul Finkelman

The Fourteenth Amendment and the Joint Committee on Reconstruction

FOR HISTORIANS, THE Fourteenth Amendment is one of the three "Civil War Amendments"—the Thirteenth, Fourteenth, and Fifteenth— that remade the nation after the Civil War. The Thirteenth ended slavery and involuntary servitude in the nation. The Fifteenth prohibited discrimination in voting on the basis of race or "previous condition of servitude." Sandwiched in between them was the Fourteenth, which is the subject of this chapter.

Over time the Fourteenth has emerged as one of the most important parts of the Constitution. Since the mid-twentieth century, the Fourteenth Amendment has emerged as a central—if not *the* central—provision in our constitutional jurisprudence. In the last half century or so, Section 1 of the amendment has been the driving engine of the judicial expansion of civil rights and civil liberties. During this period, scholars and jurists have combed the records of the Thirty-Ninth Congress, seeking a sure answer to the question of what the Fourteenth Amendment meant.

The search for the "intent" of the Fourteenth Amendment was at the center of the litigation in *Brown v. Board of Education*. In scheduling reargument for the fall of 1953, the Supreme Court asked lawyers to provide briefs on two historical issues:

> 1. What evidence is there that the Congress which submitted and the state legislatures and conventions which ratified the Fourteenth Amendment

contemplated or did not contemplate, understood or did not understand, that it would abolish segregation in the public schools?[1]

2. If neither the Congress in submitting nor the states in ratifying the Fourteenth Amendment understood that compliance with it would require the immediate abolition of segregation in the public schools, was it nevertheless the understanding of the framers of the amendment (a) that future Congresses might in the exercise of their power under Section 5 of the amendment, abolish segregation, or (b) that it would be within the judicial power, in light of future conditions, to construe the amendment as abolishing such segregation of its own force?[2]

Paraphrasing the court's questions of sixty years ago, we might ask, did the Congress in 1866 contemplate or understand that the amendment would make all forms of racial discrimination illegal?

These, of course, are "lawyer" questions rather than "historian" questions. For historians, the question of how to understand the meaning of the Fourteenth Amendment takes us beyond the debates on the floor of Congress, to ask questions about the political and social realities of the age and the context of the writing of the amendment. What events were fresh in the minds of the framers of the Fourteenth as they sought to secure the victory of the Union cause? These stories help guide us to what the supporters of the amendment in Congress had in mind when they wrote it.

An understanding of the Fourteenth Amendment begins not in the debates on the floor of Congress but in the history leading up to the amendment. One crucial aspect to our understanding of the Fourteenth Amendment is the striking changes in the law of race relations that took place across the North in the two decades before the Civil War began. Tied to this was the attempt of many Northerners, especially Republicans and those who would become Republicans, to change the law of race relations in this period. The second story is about the South, and the legal repression and brutal racial violence that took place there immediately after the Civil War ended.

These two stories complement each other. The first gives us an insight into the legal and political history that shaped Republican thought about

---

[1] Richard Kluger, *Simple Justice* (New York, 1976), p. 615, quoting *Brown v. Board of Education*, 345 U.S. at 972 (1954).

[2] Ibid.

76   *Paul Finkelman*

race and the aspirations of Republican leaders for a racially just society. Two key Republican congressional leaders in this story are Representative John A. Bingham, the primary author of Section 1 of the Fourteenth Amendment, and Representative Thaddeus Stevens of Pennsylvania, the most powerful member of the House of Representatives, who played a key role in the adoption of the Fourteenth Amendment and in the shaping of Republican policy toward race. How they felt about race—what their prewar and wartime positions were on race—helps us better understand the purpose of the Fourteenth Amendment. The second story, based on the evidence presented to the Joint Committee on Reconstruction, helps us understand what Congress struggled against in drafting Section 1 of the amendment, and thus illustrates what the Republican leadership of the Congress hoped the amendment would accomplish and what it would prevent. This history affects our understanding of how the Fourteenth Amendment was designed to protect both civil rights and civil liberties for all Americans.

Race and Law in the Antebellum North: A Prelude to the Fourteenth Amendment

The general view of antebellum Northern race relations has been shaped by an odd mixture of progressive and conservative scholarship. In the 1960s a number of scholars began to look carefully at the nature of race relations in the antebellum North and concluded that they were abysmal. Influenced by the civil rights movement in the South, scholars including Leon Litwack and Eugene Berwanger discovered that the antebellum North was not a paragon of equality. On the contrary, they discovered racism, segregation, and other forms of discrimination. Thus, Litwack asserted that on the eve of the Civil War "the northern Negro remained largely disenfranchised, segregated and economically oppressed," and, just as important, "change did not seem imminent." Similarly, in *The Frontier against Slavery*, Berwanger claimed that "discrimination against Negroes in the Middle West reached its height between 1846 and 1860, the same years in which the slavery extension controversy became most acute." Berwanger argued that "prejudice against Negroes was a factor in the development of antislavery feeling in the ante-bellum United States."[3] Even abolitionists came under attack. Jane Pease and William Pease argued that some lifelong opponents of slavery were uncomfortable in the presence of blacks, and that many abolitionists could never decide "whether the Negro was equal or inferior to the white; whether equality for the Negro should be stressed or whether it should be damped; whether civil and social rights should be granted him at once or only in the indefinite and provisional future; whether, in fact, social and civil rights should be granted or whether only civil rights should be given him."[4]

Writing in the early years of the civil rights movement, these scholars wanted to teach Northerners about their own racist past. Recognizing this past was a key to changing the nature of mid-twentieth-century race relations.

In an ironic twist, conservative scholars seized on this scholarship to reach a different conclusion. If the antebellum North was inherently racist, these scholars argued, the Congress in the 1860s and 1870s could not possibly have meant to create an integrated society. Thus, Raoul Berger claimed that the framers of the Fourteenth Amendment could not have intended to require integration or substantive equality for blacks. He asserted that the "key to an understanding of the Fourteenth Amendment is that the North was shot through with Negrophobia."[5]

It is certainly true that in most of the antebellum North full racial equality was rare. But it is also true that in this period many Republican politicians (or politicians who became Republicans) worked hard to alter race relations in order to move toward a more equal society. Many party leaders had long been working for greater equality. For example, in the years leading up to the Civil War, Republican leaders in Iowa, Wisconsin, New York, and Connecticut attempted to create equal suffrage.[6] Voting was not on the

---

[3]Leon F. Litwack, *North of Slavery: The Negro in the Free States, 1790–1860* (Chicago, 1961), pp. 279, 291; Eugene H. Berwanger, *The Frontier against Slavery: Western Anti-Negro Prejudice and the Slavery Extension Controversy* (1967; reprint ed., Urbana, Ill., 2002), pp. 1, 4.

[4]Jane H. Pease and William H. Pease, "Antislavery Ambivalence: Immediatism, Expedience, Race," *American Quarterly* 17 (1965):682, 695, reprinted in Paul Finkelman, ed., *Antislavery*, Articles on American Slavery, vol. 14 (New York, 1989), pp. 356, 369.

[5]Raoul Berger, *Government by Judiciary: The Transformation of the Fourteenth Amendment* (Cambridge, Mass., 1977), p. 10.

[6]Richard Sewell, *Ballots for Freedom: Antislavery Politics in the United States, 1837–1860* (New York, 1976), pp. 323, 333–35; Phyllis F. Field, *The Politics of Race in New York: The Struggle for*

78 Paul Finkelman

agenda in 1866, but the Republican congressional leaders who had long been working for racial equality (or something close to it) at the state level saw the Fourteenth Amendment as an opportunity to achieve this goal at the national level.

Thaddeus Stevens and Race in Pennsylvania

In 1866 Thaddeus Stevens (fig. 1) was the most powerful member of the House of Representatives, and perhaps the most powerful politician in the nation. He was also a key member of the Joint Committee on Reconstruction, which drafted the Fourteenth Amendment. In 1866, as a member of the Joint Committee, he was in a position to implement his ideology.

For more than four decades Stevens had been an uncompromising supporter of black rights and racial equality. As a delegate to the 1837 Pennsylvania Constitutional Convention, Stevens worked hard to maintain black suffrage in the face of Jacksonian Democrats, who were intent on taking the vote away from blacks. Stevens was unsuccessful in this effort. This failure, however, only increased his commitment to racial equality. From the 1820s on, Stevens regularly took fugitive slave cases for free. His most famous effort came in the dramatic prosecutions in the wake of the Christiana incident. In 1851 a slave owner, his relatives, and a U.S. deputy marshal had attempted to seize a fugitive slave living with a number of other fugitive slaves and free blacks in Christiana, Pennsylvania (fig. 2). The blacks refused to surrender peacefully and instead opened fire on the approaching whites. A short battle ensued, which left the slave owner dead and his relatives wounded. The slave who had killed his master calmly traveled by train to Rochester, New York, where he visited Frederick Douglass before taking a boat to Canada. Meanwhile, President Millard Fillmore and Secretary of State Daniel Webster insisted on treason trials, and the federal prosecutor secured indictments for treason for more than forty blacks and five white men who had refused to help the marshal arrest the fugitive slaves.[7] Part of the defense strategy included defying racial conventions; thus, the black defendants entered the courtroom accompanied by white women, to the

---

Black Suffrage in the Civil War Era (Ithaca, N.Y., 1982); Eric Foner, *Free Soil, Free Labor, Free Men: The Ideology of the Republican Party before the Civil War* (New York, 1970), p. 261.

[7] Paul Finkelman, *Millard Fillmore* (New York, 2011), pp. 119–29.

FIG. 1. Representative Thaddeus Stevens of Pennsylvania, from a photograph ca. 1860–68. *(Brady-Handy photograph collection, Library of Congress Prints and Photographs Division)*

FIG. 2. A wood engraving published in 1872 depicts African Americans firing on slave catchers near Christiana, Pennsylvania, in 1851. *(Library of Congress Prints and Photographs Division)*

horror of the proslavery prosecutors. Here, Stevens, as a key strategist in the case, demonstrated his belief in fundamental racial equality and his willingness to challenge the racial status quo.[8]

Stevens's relationships with blacks were more than political. He saw them as his social equals, and he acted on this belief in his personal life. Stevens had a longtime black housekeeper who was probably his paramour. But whatever their private relations, in public Stevens treated her with respect and dignity. "He always addressed her as 'Madam,' gave her his seat in public conveyances, and included her in social intercourse with his friends." Here, again, Stevens challenged prejudice. Indeed, throughout the last half century of his life, Stevens challenged racism. Even in death the congressman from Pennsylvania struck a blow for equality. Before he died, Stevens

---

[8]Hans L. Trefousse, *Thaddeus Stevens: Nineteenth-Century Egalitarian* (New York, 1997), pp. 174, 14–15, 49–50. After the judge in the first trial instructed the jury that the case did not amount to treason, the defendant was found not guilty and the remaining cases were dropped by the prosecution. Paul Finkelman, "The Treason Trial of Castner Hanway," in Michal R. Belknap, ed., *American Political Trials*, rev. ed. (Westport, Conn., 1994), pp. 77, 82, 84–86, 89.

made certain he would be buried in a cemetery that accepted the bodies of all people without regard to race.[9]

Race relations in Pennsylvania during Stevens's lifetime were complicated and often in flux. The high point of antebellum Northern racism was not the 1850s and the eve of the Civil War, as Litwack, Berwanger, and Berger claim. Rather, it was in the 1830s—the age of Andrew Jackson—when "Jacksonian democracy" came to mean an expansion of rights for white men and a contraction of rights for blacks. Until 1837 black men could vote in Pennsylvania, but in that year a new constitution deprived them of that right. As I have already noted, Stevens was unsuccessful in fighting this change. By the 1840s, however, the racial climate in Pennsylvania had begun to move in a more progressive direction. The South's incessant demands for more slave territories and greater federal support for slavery led to greater Northern opposition to slavery. This opposition to slavery, and Southern demands for protecting and expanding slavery, also led to greater rights and legal protections for blacks.

Even while the Jacksonians were disfranchising blacks, the state enforced its laws to protect black freedom. Laws passed at an earlier time, when Pennsylvania had been in the forefront of protecting black liberty, remained in force. Pennsylvania's 1826 Personal Liberty Law, for example, was designed to protect free blacks from kidnapping and also provide some measure of due process for alleged fugitive slaves. In 1837 a justice of the peace invoked it to prevent Edward Prigg and three other Marylanders from removing Margaret Morgan and her children from the state. Prigg and his cohorts then seized Morgan and her children without any legal authority and dragged them to Maryland. Pennsylvania authorities quickly indicted Prigg and the other Marylanders for kidnapping. Pennsylvania's governor pushed hard to have the Marylanders extradited, but ultimately Maryland returned only Prigg to Pennsylvania, where he was convicted of kidnapping. In *Prigg v. Pennsylvania*, the U.S. Supreme Court overturned Prigg's conviction and struck down the state's 1826 Personal Liberty Law. In response to this case the state withdrew all support for enforcement of the Federal Fugitive Slave Law and the Fugitive Slave Clause of the Constitution, and prohibited its officials from aiding in the return of fugitive slaves. This act also altered the state's law with regard to visiting slaves. Before 1847 a Southern master could

---

[9]Trefousse, *Thaddeus Stevens*, pp. 69, 242.

82 Paul Finkelman

bring a slave into Pennsylvania for up to six months. But after 1847 any slave brought into Pennsylvania, even for a moment, became instantly free.[10] Pennsylvania's position on the rights of free blacks and the rights of fugitive slaves and slaves in transit illustrates the complexity of race relations in that state during the time of Stevens's rise to political power. Increasingly, the state protected black liberty and offered African Americans safe haven from bondage. While Pennsylvania took the vote away from blacks in the 1830s, the state never attempted to limit their immigration or their right to own property. Had the state been as racist as some scholars argue, we could imagine new laws making black migration difficult. The 1847 repeal of the "six months law," which since 1780 had allowed visiting masters to bring slaves into the state for up to half a year, meant that any slaves brought into the state would remain there as free people. Once there, Pennsylvania blacks could own property, enter the professions, attend schools, testify against whites in court, and fully exercise their rights to freedom of speech, press, and assembly. In *Formans v. Tamm* (1853), the Pennsylvania Supreme Court ruled that blacks had the same right to own land as whites, even if they did not have the right to vote. They could also agitate for full political rights, as well as protest private discrimination. And of course they could, and did, participate in all sorts of protests against slavery.[11]

The opinion in *Formans* illustrates one aspect of the attitudes of Pennsylvanians on the eve of emancipation. Written by Ellis Lewis, a Jacksonian Democrat who was an ally of President James Buchanan, and no friend of

---

[10]Fugitive Slave Act of 1826, ch. L, 1826 Pa. Laws 150 (Pennsylvania Personal Liberty Law); *Prigg v. Pennsylvania*, 41 U.S. (16 Pet.) 539 (1842); Paul Finkelman, *Supreme Injustice: Slavery in the Nation's Highest Court* (Cambridge, Mass., 2018), pp. 140–71; Paul Finkelman, "Story Telling on the Supreme Court: *Prigg v. Pennsylvania* and Justice Joseph Story's Judicial Nationalism," *Supreme Court Review* 1994 (1994):247; Paul Finkelman, "*Prigg v. Pennsylvania* and Northern State Courts: Anti-slavery Use of a Pro-slavery Decision," *Civil War History* 25 (1979):5; Act of Mar. 3, 1847, ch. 159, 1847 Pa. Laws 206–8 (preventing kidnapping, preserving the public peace, and prohibiting the exercise of certain powers previously exercised by judges, and to repeal certain slave laws). See generally Paul Finkelman, *An Imperfect Union: Slavery, Federalism, and Comity* (Chapel Hill, N.C., 1981), pp. 137–39 (discussing the evolution of law in the North from allowing masters to visit free states while accompanied by slaves to immediately freeing all slaves voluntarily brought into free states).

[11]Act of Mar. 1, 1780, ch. CXLVI, 1780 Pa. Laws 296 (allowing visiting masters to keep slaves in the state for up to six months), repealed by Act of Mar. 3, 1847, ch. 159, 1847 Pa. Laws 206–8; *Formans v. Tamm*, 1 Grant 23 (Pa. 1853) (upholding black property rights in Pennsylvania). See also Paul Finkelman, "Human Liberty, Property in Human Beings, and the Pennsylvania Supreme Court," *Duquesne Law Review* 53 (2015):453–82.

abolition, the opinion nevertheless supported some of the fundamental rights of "equal protection" of the law that would be enshrined in the Fourteenth Amendment. Justice Lewis argued that "the effect" of ending slavery in Pennsylvania was

> to give to the colored man the right to acquire, possess and dispose of lands and goods, as fully as the white man enjoys these rights. Having no one to look to for support but himself, it would be a mockery to tell him he is a "free man," if he be not allowed the necessary means of sustaining life. The right to the fruits of his industry and to invest them in lands or goods, or in such manner as he may deem most conducive to his comfort, is an incident to the grant of his freedom.[12]

Immediately after the Civil War, former Confederate states would in fact enact such laws that mocked the ending of slavery, to prevent blacks from having basic common-law rights and in many places denying them the right to rent or own land. Thus, the experience in Pennsylvania, even coming from antiabolitionist jurists, was that blacks, including former slaves, had to have equal protection of the law.

During the late antebellum period, Pennsylvania's government turned a blind eye to the active involvement of blacks and whites in the underground railroad, which of course led to more blacks coming to Pennsylvania and remaining in the state. On the other hand, state officials continued to prosecute whites accused of kidnapping free blacks.[13] Meanwhile, in increasing numbers the people of Pennsylvania voted for antislavery politicians such as Stevens, Simon Cameron, and William D. "Pig Iron" Kelly, who were ready to fight against human bondage and for human equality.

These experiences and this history shaped the background that Stevens brought to Congress and to the Joint Committee on Reconstruction, which drafted the Fourteenth Amendment.

---

[12]*Formans*, p. 25.

[13]Act of Mar. 3, 1847, ch. 159, 1847 Pa. Laws 206–8 (denying state support for recapturing fugitive slaves); William Still, *The Underground Railroad* (1872; reprint ed., New York, 1968). See, e.g., *Commonwealth v. Auld*, 4 Pa. L.J. 515 (1850) (charging a master with the kidnapping of his runaway slave's children); *A Review of the Trial, Conviction, and Sentence of George Alberti, for Kidnapping* [1851] and *The Trial of Emanual Myers, of Maryland, for Kidnapping Certain Fugitive Slaves, Had at Carlisle, Pennsylvania, November, 1859* [1859], both reprinted in Paul Finkelman, ed., *Fugitive Slaves and the American Courts: The Pamphlet Literature*, Slavery, Race, and the American Legal System, 16 vols. (New York, 1988), 2:27, 4:121.

John A. Bingham and Race Relations in Ohio

The experience of Congressman John A. Bingham of Ohio (fig. 3) mirrors that of Stevens.[14] Like Stevens, Bingham served on the Joint Committee on Reconstruction. Bingham, the author of Section 1 of the Fourteenth Amendment, was equally a longtime opponent of racial discrimination. And like Stevens, he had fought against slavery and segregation. In his home state of Ohio, Bingham had witnessed a dramatic change in the nature of race relations. In the first decades of the nineteenth century, Ohio was one of the most racially retrograde states in the North. However, by the 1840s this had begun to change, and this change continued through the 1850s as Bingham's new political organization, the Republican Party, gained power.

In 1804 and 1807 Ohio adopted elaborate registration requirements for blacks entering the state. These laws were rarely enforced and were utterly ineffective in limiting the growth of the state's free black community. Indeed, while these laws were on the books Ohio's black population grew rapidly. Nevertheless, these laws always posed a threat to blacks, who might be forced out of the state if they could not prove their freedom or find sureties to promise to support them if they were unable to support themselves. Ohio also prevented blacks from voting, serving on juries, and testifying against whites. Ohio prohibited blacks from attending schools with whites while denying them meaningful access to public schools, even on a segregated basis. Such laws were what led Raoul Berger to argue that the antebellum North was "shot through with Negrophobia."[15]

However, in Ohio and other parts of the North there was a profound transformation of the law with regard to race in the last two antebellum

---

[14]On Bingham, see generally, Gerard N. Magliocca, *American Founding Son: John Bingham and the Invention of the Fourteenth Amendment* (New York, 2013).

[15]In 1800 Ohio had a black population of 337; it had grown by more than 550 percent to 1,899 by 1810, despite the fact that anti-immigration laws were on the books for six of those years. It more than doubled to 4,723 in the next decade, and doubled again in the next decade, reaching 9,568 by 1830; by 1840 the black population was 17,342, and in 1850, a year after the registration laws went off the books, the census found 25,279 blacks in the state, giving it the third-largest free black population in the North. See United States Census, *Negro Population, 1790–1915* (Washington, D.C., 1915), p. 57. Ohio Constitution of 1802, Art. IV, Sec. 1 (limiting the franchise to white males); Act of Feb. 9, 1831, 29 Ohio Laws 94 (1831) (relating to juries); Act of Jan. 25, 1807, 5 Ohio Laws 53 (1807) (amending the act of Jan. 5, 1804, entitled "An Act Regulating Black and Mulatto Persons"); Act of Feb. 10, 1829, 27 Ohio Laws 72 (1829) (providing "for the support and better regulation of common schools"). Berger, *Government by Judiciary*, p. 10.

FIG. 3. Representative John A. Bingham of Ohio, from a photograph ca. 1860–75. *(Brady-Handy photograph collection, Library of Congress Prints and Photographs Division)*

86 *Paul Finkelman*

decades. This change was especially apparent in Ohio, at precisely the time that Bingham, Salmon P. Chase, Jacob Brinkerhoff, James Ashley, and other future leaders of the Ohio Republican Party were entering politics or taking a leading role in the state's new Republican Party.[16]

In 1839 the state legislature created an elaborate system for regulating the return of fugitive slaves. The law required that ownership of a fugitive slave "be proved" to the "satisfaction" of a state judge while at the same time authorizing state officials to aid in the return of bona fide fugitive slaves.[17] This law was consistent with Ohio's long-standing policy of protecting free blacks from kidnapping while supporting its constitutional obligation to return fugitive slaves. However, unlike earlier laws that only punished kidnapping after it had occurred, this act had the potential to frustrate attempts by masters to recover fugitive slaves as well as stopping kidnapping. Thus, the law would have made fugitives feel more secure in the Buckeye State because it gave blacks greater protections.

The adoption of this law cuts against the idea of a "negrophobic" Ohio, because the end result of the law was to increase the black population and make the state a haven for runaway slaves. If Ohio had been truly "negrophobic" it would have done everything it could to discourage blacks from living in the state. Under such a policy Ohio would have withheld specific legislative protection from free blacks, and instead of creating barriers to the return of fugitives, it would have provided legislation to help slave catchers. A truly negrophobic Ohio would have passed laws similar to those in the South, which required law enforcement officers to incarcerate black strangers and travelers and advertise them as runaway slaves unless they could document their status as free people.

---

[16]Brinkerhoff (1810–1880) became a county prosecutor in 1839 and served in Congress as an antislavery Democrat from 1843 to 1847. He was a Free Soil member of the legislature in the late 1840s and joined the Ohio Republican Party when it was formed in 1856. He was a state supreme court justice from 1856 to 1871. Others in this cohort included Edward Wade (1802–1866), a Free Soil and Republican member of Congress from 1853 to 1861; Benjamin F. Wade (1800–1878), who entered politics in 1835 and became a powerful figure as a state senator, judge, and then U.S. senator in the 1840s and 1850s; James Ashley (1824–1896), who entered politics in 1858, serving as a Republican member of Congress; and William Dennison Jr. (1815–1882), who served as governor of Ohio from 1860 to 1862 and as postmaster general from 1864 to July 1866.

[17]Act of Feb. 26, 1839, ch. 37, 1838 Ohio Laws 38 (relating to fugitives from labor or service from other states). For a general history of these laws, and others in Ohio, see Stephen Middleton, *The Black Laws: Race and the Legal Process in Early Ohio* (Athens, 2005).

The Joint Committee on Reconstruction 87

As noted above, in *Prigg v. Pennsylvania* the U.S. Supreme Court barred any state from regulating the return of fugitive slaves. This decision struck down the personal liberty laws of the free states, like Ohio's 1839 Act. In response to *Prigg*, the Ohio legislature repealed the 1839 Act in 1843 and reinstated an earlier law, which provided imprisonment "at hard labor" for up to seven years for anyone convicted of removing a free black from the state as a fugitive slave or even attempting to seize a free black with the intent to remove that person from the state.[18] Again, a negrophobic state would not have passed a new law to punish the kidnapping of free blacks.

Starting in 1848—at a time when Bingham was beginning his political career as the district attorney of Tuscarawas County—Ohio began to rapidly change its racial laws while taking an increasingly strong stand against Southern slavery. A resolution of that year urged the national Congress to prohibit slavery in any territories acquired in the Mexican War. More significantly for the background to the Fourteenth Amendment, in that year a new law provided two separate methods for the education of blacks. The law for the first time specifically allowed school districts to permit blacks to attend schools with whites. The law also authorized the creation of segregated schools for blacks funded by taxes collected from blacks. These schools would be organized on a segregated basis. While considered a mark of discrimination at the time (just as it is today), this law was nevertheless an important and positive step forward in the expansion of rights for blacks in Ohio. Without this legal provision, blacks had no right to a public education, on either an integrated or a segregated basis. This law marked an improvement over these earlier conditions that denied blacks access to a public education. In addition, it allowed blacks to attend schools with whites, if local communities did not object. An 1849 law repealed the registration and surety bond requirements of the earlier laws, allowed blacks to testify against whites, and gave them even greater access to the public schools.[19] Laws

---

[18]"An Act to Repeal the Act Entitled, 'An Act Relating to Fugitives from Labor and Service from Other States,'" Act of Jan. 19, 1843, *Ohio Laws of 1842*, 41:13.

[19]"Resolution Declaring That So Much of the Ordinance of 1787 as Relating to Slavery, Should Be Extended to the Territory Acquired from Mexico," Resolution of Feb. 25, 1848, *Ohio Laws of 1847*, vol. 46: 314; "An Act to Provide for the Establishment of Common Schools for the Education of Children of Black and Mulatto Persons, and Amending the March 7, 1838 Act Entitled, 'An Act for the Support and Better Regulation of Common Schools, and to Create Permanently the Office of superintendent,'" Act of Feb. 24, 1848, *Ohio Laws of 1847*, vol. 46: 81; "An Act to Authorize the Establishment of

88   *Paul Finkelman*

adopted by Ohio in the 1850s, when Bingham was representing his state in Congress, provided blacks with new protections against kidnapping and demonstrated Ohio's hostility to the Fugitive Slave Law of 1850.

By the eve of the Civil War, blacks did not have full equality in Ohio. They still could not vote, serve on juries, or serve in the state militia (although this was a result of existing federal law). But, they had far more legal rights than they ever had before. Moreover, the thrust of the newly created Republican Party was toward greater racial equality. Far from being "shot through with Negrophobia," Ohio in this period was making steady and significant progress toward a more egalitarian polity that provided increasing rights for free blacks. Ohio did not entirely eliminate discriminatory laws at this time, because a substantial number of voters were Democrats who opposed racial equality and were later hostile to emancipation. After antislavery Democrats such as Chase and Brinkerhoff joined the new Republican Party, the Democrats became extremely hostile to blacks. These Democratic voters and their representatives in the state legislature, who were particularly powerful in southern Ohio, were able to block some changes, especially those requiring a constitutional amendment. They were also able to block Republican hegemony in the 1850s and 1860s, and sometimes the Democrats controlled the state legislature. Ohio in the late antebellum period was a divided polity, with the Republicans usually, but not always, able to control state government.

It was in the context of these statutes and court decisions, as well as executive actions against slavery, that John Bingham became a key member of the Ohio Republican Party and a rising star in national politics. His pedigree was deeply connected to antislavery and black civil rights. He brought these ideas to Congress and to his role in drafting the Fourteenth Amendment.

When we consider what the amendment meant, we must begin with the backgrounds and experiences of key Republican leaders like Stevens and Bingham. We must further consider the racial trajectory of the North—and

---

Separate Schools for the Education of Colored Children, and for Other Purposes," Act of Feb. 10, 1849, *Ohio Laws of 1848*, vol. 47: 17. See Howard N. Rabinowitz, "More Than the Woodward Thesis: Assessing the Strange Career of Jim Crow," *Journal of American History* 75 (1988):842 (discussing this issue in the post–Civil War South). Rabinowitz "discovered" that what preceded segregation in the South "was normally exclusion" and that "ironically, segregation often therefore marked an improvement in the status of blacks." Ibid., p. 845.

more significantly the Republican Party in the North. The evidence suggests that for Stevens, Bingham, and other Republicans, black civil rights mattered.[20]

The key to understanding Bingham's Ohio background is that parts of his state were clearly negrophobic, but that in his northern Ohio district, and in much of the state, Free Soilers and Republicans gained enormous power in the late 1840s and 1850s. These Republicans won elections while expanding the rights and liberties of blacks in Ohio. By the mid-1860s they were at their zenith of political power, and they brought with them a long history of civil rights advocacy as well as a track record of successfully moving Ohio forward in the march to civil rights.

The Southern Context of Reconstruction and the Shaping of the Fourteenth Amendment

Stevens, Bingham, and other Republicans in the Thirty-Ninth Congress were influenced not only by their own long struggle against racism in the North and slavery in the South. The retrograde actions of Southern politicians and the racist brutality of Southern whites in the wake of the Civil War also affected their constitutional views. A brief description of race relations in the South in 1865–66 reminds us of why the Fourteenth Amendment was passed and helps us understand what Stevens, Bingham, and their Republican colleagues hoped it would accomplish.

The Aftermath of Slavery

In April 1865 the United States successfully suppressed what leaders at the time referred to as "the late wicked Rebellion." The suppression of the rebellion involved more than two million soldiers and sailors, 10 percent of whom were African Americans. The majority of these black men in uniform—the "sable arm" of the U.S. Army and Navy—had been slaves

---

[20]See *Commonwealth v. Dennison*, 65 U.S. (24 How.) 66, 68–69 (1861) (holding that the federal Constitution does not impose an obligation on one state to "surrender its citizens or residents to any other state on the charge that they have committed an offence not known to the laws of the former"). Republicans in New York and Connecticut, for example, attempted to create equal suffrage in their state.

90   *Paul Finkelman*

when the rebellion began. Most Northerners understood that these black soldiers had earned their freedom and a claim to political and legal equality. Republican politicians like Stevens and Bingham assumed the end of slavery would lead to a new political reality in the South that would include the votes of the freedmen, as the former slaves were called. In much of the South, blacks constituted a third to a half of the population. These Republican leaders venerated and celebrated the idea of a "Republican form of government" (as the Constitution required), in which the people of a society elected a legislature and in which all citizens had equal rights under the law. Thus, Northern politicians expected that emancipation, which was completed with the ratification of the Thirteenth Amendment in December 1865, would lead to more than simply an end to slavery: they assumed it would lead to an entire revolution in the way blacks were treated and in the rights they had.[21]

Southern whites, however, had other ideas. General Carl Schurz, after visiting the South in 1865, concluded that many, perhaps most, Southern whites conceded that blacks were no longer the slaves of individual masters but intended to make them "the slaves of society."[22]

The following fall, Southern voters—all of whom were white and most of whom had supported the rebellion—elected new state legislatures. Many of these state lawmakers had served in the Confederate government or in the rebellious state governments. Others had been soldiers—often officers— in the traitorous Confederate army. The majority had been either slave owners or members of slave-owning families. Although defeated in battle and deprived of their slaves by a combination of congressional acts, the Emancipation Proclamation, the brilliant military success of the U.S. Army, and the Thirteenth Amendment, these former Confederates were unwilling to accept that the war had fundamentally altered the racial status quo in the South. They knew that African Americans could no longer be held as chattel

---

[21] *Ex parte Milligan*, 71 U.S. (4 Wall.) 2, 16 (1866). See David Dudley Cornish, *The Sable Arm: Negro Troops in the Union Army, 1861–1865* (New York, 1966), pp. 29, 184. Clearly, most midcentury Americans saw no contradiction between the idea of the republican form of government and the denial of suffrage to women. At the time most men—and many women—would have defended this result, agreeing that women were effectively represented by their adult male relatives. Thus the failure to enfranchise women did not violate the republican form of government clause of the constitution. Obviously proponents of women's suffrage, such as Elizabeth Cady Stanton, would have rejected this analysis.
[22] Richard N. Current, ed., *Reconstruction 1865–1877* (Englewood Cliffs, N.J., 1965), p. 38.

slaves, to be bought and sold at the whim of a master; but they were unprepared to accept that the freedmen were entitled to liberty, equality, or even fundamental legal rights. Many Northerners were shocked by the statutes that unreconstructed Southern legislatures passed immediately after the war. The statutes indicated how the South planned to treat the former slaves. The Fourteenth Amendment was in large part a reaction to these laws, generally known as black codes.

The Joint Committee on Reconstruction

In December 1865 Congress created the Joint Committee on Reconstruction to investigate conditions in the South. The Joint Committee consisted of six senators and nine representatives. Thaddeus Stevens and John Bingham were key House members on the committee. Also on the committee were George S. Boutwell of Massachusetts and Justin Morrill of Vermont. Both had been lifelong opponents of slavery, and both came from states that gave free blacks full legal rights, including suffrage. The work of this committee led to the Civil Rights Act of 1866, reported out of the committee on April 30, 1866, and to the proposed Fourteenth Amendment, which Congress passed on June 13, 1866. Eleven members signed the final report. Three Southerners and a New Jersey Democrat refused to sign the report.

This massive report was nearly 800 pages long. The committee members interviewed scores of people—former slaves, former Confederate leaders and slave owners, U.S. Army officers, journalists, Northern ministers, and others in the South. In its report the committee reminded the nation that the former slaves had "remained true and loyal" throughout the Civil War and "in large numbers, fought on the side of the Union." The committee concluded that it would be impossible to "abandon" the former slaves "without securing them their rights as free men and citizens." Indeed, the "whole civilized world would have cried out against such base ingratitude" if the U.S. government failed to secure and protect the rights of the freedpeople. The committee also found that Southern leaders still "defend[ed] the legal right of secession, and [upheld] the doctrine that the first allegiance of the people is due to the States." Noting the "leniency" of the policies of Congress and the president after the war, the committee discovered that "[i]n return for our leniency we receive only an insulting denial of our authority." Rather than accept the outcome of the war, Southern whites were using local courts to

92 Paul Finkelman

prosecute loyalists and "Union officers for acts done in the line of official duty," and "similar prosecutions" were "threatened elsewhere as soon as the United States troops [we]re removed."[23]

The committee understood that the task before the Congress and the nation involved three things: preventing former Confederates from reinstating the same type of regime that existed before the war, protecting the liberty of former slaves and guaranteeing them the power to protect their own rights within the new political regime that had to be created, and protecting the rights and safety of white Unionists who were threatened by the violence of as yet unreconstructed Southern whites who had not accepted the political or social outcome of the war. After investigating the situation in the South, the committee concluded that nothing short of a constitutional amendment— what became the Fourteenth Amendment—would protect the rights of the former slaves.

Two categories of evidence were particularly important in setting out the need for civil rights legislation and a constitutional amendment to protect liberty in the states. The Joint Committee learned a good deal about conditions in the South by examining the statutes and constitutions adopted by the former Confederate states immediately after the war. In addition, the Joint Committee interviewed hundreds of people familiar with conditions in the postwar South. The information from these interviews, along with some published materials, such as excerpts from Southern state constitutions, filled the nearly 800 pages of the Joint Committee's report. Both the legal documentation and the evidence from interviews led to the inescapable conclusion that the majority of Southern whites were not prepared to accept blacks as equal citizens and that many Southern whites were willing to use intimidation, violence, and murder to prevent racial equality in the postwar South.

The Black Codes and State Constitutions, 1865–66

The Southern black codes and constitutions passed in 1865 and 1866 were designed to replicate, as closely as possible, the prewar suppression and

---

[23] *Report of the Joint Committee on Reconstruction*, 39th Cong., 1st sess., 1866, *Resolution and Report of the Committee*, pp. xiii, xvii–xviii (hereafter cited as *Report of the Joint Committee*, with a reference to the particular part or section and page numbers).

exploitation of blacks. The Alabama Black Code of 1865–66 began by acknowledging the new status of blacks, declaring that "[a]ll freedmen, free negroes, and mulattoes" had "the right to sue and be sued, plead and be impleaded." Slaves had never had these rights. The law also allowed blacks to testify in court, "but only in cases in which freedmen, free negroes and mulattoes are parties, either as plaintiff or defendant." In addition, blacks were allowed to testify in prosecutions "for injuries in the persons and property" of blacks.[24] Mississippi enacted similar legislation, which more directly and unambiguously provided that blacks could testify against white criminal defendants "in all criminal prosecutions where the crime charged is alleged to have been committed by a white person upon or against the person or property of a freedman, free negro, or mulatto."[25]

These laws certainly expanded the rights of Southern blacks and gave them some legal protections they had not had before the war. For the first time in the history of these states, blacks could testify against whites. However, such laws did not give blacks the same legal rights as whites. Under these laws, blacks could not testify in a suit between two whites or at the prosecution of a white for harming other whites. Thus, the law in effect declared that blacks were not "equal" to whites and that their testimony was not as "good" as that of whites. These restrictions undermined fundamental justice and created dangerous possibilities for free blacks and their white allies. For example, a white suing another white could not use the testimony of a black to support his case. More importantly, under these laws Southern white terrorists could kill a white in front of black witnesses, and those witnesses could not testify at the trial. This would undermine the safety of those white teachers, army officers, Freedmen's Bureau officers, and Unionists who supported black rights and the national government. Thus, while these new laws gave some protection to blacks, the laws did not give them legal equality and they did not even fully protect their civil rights.

The laws allowing blacks to sign contacts and to sue and be sued under them appear, at first glance, to support black freedom, but in fact they undermined black rights. Before the war, slaves had no rights to sign contracts, and some slave states limited the rights of free blacks to enter into contracts.

---

[24]Ibid., p. xvii.
[25]Act of Nov. 25, 1865, ch. 4, 1865 Mississippi Laws 82 ("An Act for Conferring Civil Rights on Freedmen, and for Other Purposes").

94   *Paul Finkelman*

Certainly laws allowing blacks to enter into contracts appear to be a concession to black freedom since they gave the freedmen rights they had never had as slaves. Such basic economic rights were vital to freedom, and they were rights that slaves had never had. Thus, on the surface, the laws granting former slaves the right to enter into contracts were an important sign of freedom. But in fact, these laws dramatically threatened blacks' civil rights.

Former slaves in the Deep South were almost universally illiterate, had virtually no experience with either the law or a free economy, and were only a few months out of slavery. They were vulnerable to signing contracts—which would involve their "mark" or an "x"—that committed them to long-term labor agreements, and to being sued for breach of these contracts if they could not fulfill them. Some of the laws provided that blacks who did not fulfill a contract for any reason could be sued and forced to work for free to pay damages, or be denied any pay for work done if they left their job—no matter what the reason—before the end of the contract. The terms of the contracts were almost always completely favorable to the white employer and exploitative of the black worker. These laws encouraged planters to exploit and abuse black workers, especially near the end of a contract term, in hopes that these workers would leave and would not have to be paid or might be forced to work for free to pay damages under the contract. Laws similar to those in Mississippi were found in other states. Thus, Major General Christopher C. Andrews told the Joint Committee on Reconstruction that conditions in Texas were such that "[u]nless the freedmen are protected by the government they will be much worse off than when they were slaves" because the whites were prepared "to coerce" blacks into working for unfair wages under unfair contracts.[26]

Other provisions of the black laws more blatantly undermined black freedom. Alabama's law "Concerning Vagrants and Vagrancy" allowed for the incarceration in the public workhouse of any "laborer or servant who loiters away his time, or refuses to comply with any contract for a term of service without just cause."[27] Mississippi's Civil Rights Act of 1865 provided that if any laborer quit a job before the end of the contract period he would

---

[26] *Report of the Joint Committee*, Part IV: Florida, Louisiana, Texas, p. 125.

[27] Act of Nov. 24, 1865, ch. 6, 1865 Alabama Laws 90 ("An Act for Amending the Vagrant Laws of the State").

lose all wages earned up to that time. Thus, if a black laborer signed a contract to work for a planter for a year but left after eleven months, he would get no wages. This provision allowed employers to mistreat and overwork laborers, including whipping them as had been done under slavery, knowing they dare not quit. Indeed, a shrewd employer could purposefully make life miserable for workers near the end of a contract term, in hopes that they would quit and forfeit all wages. Mississippi law further declared that any blacks "with no lawful employment or business" would be considered vagrants and could be fined up to fifty dollars. Blacks who could not pay the fine would be forcibly hired out to whoever would pay the fine, thus creating another form of unfree labor. The same act created a one dollar poll tax for all free blacks. Anyone not paying the tax could also be declared a vagrant and thus assigned to some white planter to work at hard labor.[28] These laws also prohibited blacks from renting land or houses in towns or cities, thus in effect forcing blacks into the countryside, where they were doomed to agricultural labor.

Laws such as these set the stage for a new system of forced labor. Southern states passed these laws just before, or immediately after, the ratification of the Thirteenth Amendment. They were attempts to reduce blacks to a status somewhere between that of slaves (which they no longer were) and full free people (which the white South would not allow). The labor contract laws, tied to the vagrancy laws, were designed to create a kind of serfdom, tying the former slaves to the land, just as they were once tied to their masters.

The new state constitutions were equally oppressive. The Joint Committee reprinted some state constitutions and excerpts from others in its report.[29] The Florida Constitution, for example, limited suffrage to whites and prohibited any person employed by the United States—white or black— from voting in the state unless he was a resident of Florida before entering federal service. The same constitution prohibited blacks from serving as jurors and limited their testimony to cases involving blacks.[30] The Arkansas Constitution similarly limited voting to whites, banned federal officers

---

[28]Act of Nov. 25, 1865, ch. 4, 1865 Mississippi Laws 82, 90 ("An Act for Conferring Civil Rights on Freedmen, and for Other Purposes").

[29]*Report of the Joint Committee, Resolution and Report of the Committee*, pp. iv–vi.

[30]*Report of the Joint Committee*, Part IV: Florida, Louisiana, Texas, p. 26.

96 *Paul Finkelman*

from voting, and discriminated against blacks in other ways.[31] The Georgia Constitution was similar, limiting the vote to whites. The state used a statute to limit black testimony. This too was included in the committee report.[32] These laws and constitutional provisions astounded Northerners. Having been defeated in battle and forced to give up slavery, the South seemed as defiant as ever, unwilling to accept the outcome of the war and the necessity of treating blacks as citizens. The reaction to these laws led to the Civil Rights Act of 1866 and to the Fourteenth Amendment.

Southern White Attacks on Blacks and the Report of the Joint Committee on Reconstruction

The Southern black codes were not the only cause of Northern astonishment at Southern behavior. Even more important, perhaps, was the violence directed at blacks and their white allies after the war.

While Congress debated what became the Civil Rights Act of 1866, Senator Charles Sumner of Massachusetts received a box containing the finger of a black man. The accompanying note read: "You old son of a bitch, I send you a piece of one of your friends, and if that bill of yours passes I will have a piece of you."[33] This box and note illustrated all too well the murderous and lethal violence that Southern whites were prepared to use to suppress black freedom.

The evidence presented in the massive committee report documented the dangers to blacks and white Unionists—and the nation itself—posed by the refusal of most former Confederates to accept black freedom. Congressman Bingham chaired the subcommittee that investigated the situation in Tennessee. Everyone agreed that Tennessee had more Union supporters than any other former Confederate state, and in the end the committee endorsed its immediate readmission to the Union.[34] Nevertheless, a sampling of the testimony gathered from Tennessee supports the understanding that

---

[31] *Report of the Joint Committee*, Part III: Georgia, Alabama, Mississippi, Arkansas, pp. 85–86.

[32] *Report of the Joint Committee*, Part III: Georgia, Alabama, Mississippi, Arkansas, p. 186.

[33] James M. McPherson, *The Struggle for Equality: Abolitionists and the Negro in the Civil War and Reconstruction* (Princeton, N.J., 2014), p. 341.

[34] *Report of the Joint Committee on Reconstruction, Resolution and Report of the Committee* xix; *Report of the Joint Committee on Reconstruction*, Part I: Tennessee, title page and pp. 93, 107.

the committee that wrote the Fourteenth Amendment was fully aware of the need for a powerful weapon to force change and protect freedom in the South. Testimony from other states reveals that the rest of the South was even more prone to violence toward blacks and Unionists, and that liberty was even more imperiled elsewhere in the former Confederacy.

Major General Edward Hatch testified that throughout Tennessee whites were unwilling to accept black liberty. General Hatch noted that "the negro is perfectly willing to work, but he wants a guarantee that he will be secured in his rights under his contract" and that "his life and property" would be "secured." Blacks understood they were "not safe from the poor whites." He noted that whites wanted "some kind of legislation" to "establish a kind of peonage; not absolute slavery but that they can enact such laws as will enable them to manage the negro as they please—to fix the price to be paid for his labor." And if blacks resisted this reestablishment of bondage, "[t]hey are liable to be shot."[35]

Major General Clinton Fisk, for whom one of the nation's first black colleges—Fisk University in Nashville, Tennessee—would be named, testified about the murderous nature of former "slaveholders and returned rebel soldiers." Such men "persecute bitterly" the former slaves, "and pursue them with vengeance, and treat them with brutality, and burn down their dwellings and school-houses." Fisk pointed out this was "not the rule" everywhere in Tennessee, but nevertheless such conduct existed.[36] And, as everyone admitted, Tennessee was the most progressive state on these issues in the former Confederacy.

Lieutenant Colonel R. W. Barnard was far less optimistic than Major General Fisk. Perhaps because he was a field officer, Barnard was more likely to see the day-to-day dangers blacks faced. Asked if it was safe to remove troops from Tennessee, he replied, "I hardly know how to express myself on the subject. I have not been in a favor of removing the military. I can tell you what an old citizen, a Union man, said to me. Said he, 'I tell you what, if you take away the military from Tennessee, the buzzards can't eat up the niggers as fast as we'll kill 'em.'" Barnard thought this might be an exaggeration but told the committee, "I know there are plenty of bad men there

---

[35] *Report of the Joint Committee on Reconstruction*, Part I: Tennessee, pp. 107–8.
[36] Ibid., pp. 112, 120–21.

98 *Paul Finkelman*

who would maltreat the negro."[37] He did not need to emphasize that this threat to black life came not from a "bad" man but from a Unionist.

Thus, in Tennessee, where loyal Union men were more common than elsewhere in the South, the dangers to blacks were great. In other states the dangers were extraordinarily greater. Major General John W. Turner reported that in Virginia "all of the [white] people" were "extremely reluctant to grant to the negro his civil rights—those privileges that pertain to freedom, the protection of life, liberty, and property before the laws, the right to testify in courts, etc." Turner noted that whites were "reluctant even to consider and treat the negro as a free man, to let him have his half of the sidewalk or the street crossing." They would only "concede" such rights to blacks "if it is ever done, because they are forced to do it." He noted that poor whites were "disposed to ban the negro, to kick him and cuff him, and threaten him." George B. Smith, a Virginia farmer, admitted that whites in the state "maltreat [blacks] every day" and that blacks had "[n]ot a particle" of a chance "to obtain justice in the civil courts of Virginia." He declared that a black or "a Union man" had as much chance of obtaining justice in Virginia as "a rabbit would in a den of lions." Others in Virginia explained over and over again how the whites were trying to reduce blacks to servitude with laws and violence. The white sheriff of Fairfax County noted that the state was "passing laws" to "disfranchise" black voters and "passing vagrant laws on purpose to oppress the colored people and to keep them in vassalage, and doing everything they can to bring back things of their old condition, as near as possible."[38]

Perhaps the most powerful testimony on Virginia came from U.S. District Judge John C. Underwood, who had lived in the state since the 1840s. He described the cold-blooded murder of a white Unionist by a returning Confederate officer. The state did not prosecute anyone for the crime. He also noted that the murderer of an army officer had "not yet been punished" but was "still at large." He believed that white Unionists in Virginia were even more vulnerable than blacks because the army would intercede to protect the freedmen, while "a Union man could" not "expect to obtain justice in the courts of the State." But if the army abandoned the state and left the fate of the freedmen to the native whites of Virginia, the situation would

---

[37] Ibid., p. 121.
[38] Ibid., Part II: Virginia, North Carolina, South Carolina, pp. 4, 5, 17, 35.

be radically altered. Judge Underwood quoted a "most intelligent" man from Alexandria who declared that "sooner than see the colored people raised to a legal and political equality, the Southern people would prefer their total annihilation."[39]

Testimony about North Carolina revealed the lethal danger to blacks in the South. A black was shot down in cold blood near Camden. A U.S. Army captain reported "numerous cases" of the "maltreatment of blacks," including flogging and shooting, and that "instances of cruelty were numerous." He predicted that without U.S. troops, schoolhouses for blacks would be burned and teachers harassed. A minister in Goldsborough reported the cold-blooded shooting of a black man in order to take his horse. When another former slave led soldiers to the culprit, this black was also murdered.[40]

Lieutenant Colonel Dexter H. Clapp told the committee about a gang of North Carolina whites who "first castrated" and then "murdered" a black man, but when the culprits escaped from jail the local police refused to even attempt to capture them. This gang then shot "several negroes." One of these men, a wealthy planter, later killed a twelve-year-old black boy and wounded another. A local police sergeant "brutally wounded a freedman . . . in his custody." While the man's arms were tied behind his back, the policeman struck him on the back of his head with a gun. It was later shown that this man had "committed no offence whatever." This policeman later "whipped another freedman" so that "from his neck to his hips his back was one mass of gashes." The policeman left the bleeding man outside all night. A black man who defended himself when assaulted by a white was given twenty-two lashes with a whip over a two-hour period, then "tied up by his thumbs for two hours, his toes touching the ground only," then "given nine more lashes and then tied up by his thumbs for another two hours." A planter in the same area whipped two black women until their backs were "a mass of gashes." Clapp asserted that away from military posts "scenes like these" were "frequent occurrences" in "portions" of North Carolina.[41]

In South Carolina, Brigadier General Rufus Saxton, who had been awarded the Congressional Medal of Honor for his wartime valor, reported numerous atrocities. In Edgefield local whites treated free people as if they

---

[39]Ibid., p. 7.
[40]Ibid., pp. 198, 202, 203, 206.
[41]Ibid., pp. 209–11.

100 Paul Finkelman

were slaves. One "freedman [and] three children, two male and one female, were stripped naked, tied up, and whipped severely," while a woman was given a hundred lashes while tied to a tree. Another man was whipped with a stick, while two children were also whipped. Saxton reported shootings, whippings (including of naked women), various forms of torture, floggings, and beatings of all kinds. In addition to attacks on blacks by individual planters, ruffians, and gangs, Saxton reported a more ominous trend: "organized bands of 'regulators'—armed men—who make it their business to traverse these counties, and maltreat negroes without any avowedly definite purpose in view. They treat the negroes, in many instances, in the most horrible and atrocious manner, even to maiming them, cutting their ears off, etc."[42]

The committee heard similar stories from Major General George Armstrong Custer, who was stationed in Texas. He reported that whites in that state blamed the black man for "their present condition," and thus they did not "hesitate" to use "every opportunity to inflict injuries upon him in order, seemingly, to punish him for this." Custer noted that in Texas more than 500 former Confederates had been charged with murdering blacks or white Unionists, but no one had been convicted. Blacks, however, were routinely convicted and jailed for minor offenses. Custer reported that "it is of a weekly, if not of a daily, occurrence that freedmen are murdered. Their bodies are found in different parts of the country," but no whites were ever charged in these cases, even when they were known. Custer reported that "[c]ases have occurred of white men meeting freedmen they never saw before, and murdering them merely from this feeling of hostility to them as a class."[43]

Testimony about the rest of the South mirrored the violence and denial of rights sketched out here. Blacks disappeared and were beaten, maimed, and killed. Legislatures passed laws to prevent them from owning land, moving to towns, voting, testifying in court, or in any other way asserting and protecting their rights as free people. The committee heard numbing reports of violence and hatred.

Perhaps even more horrible than the fear of violence was the threat of reenslavement. Brigadier General Charles H. Howard, who was serving as an inspector for the Freedmen's Bureau, reported instances in Georgia of blacks being held on plantations against their will and of others being

---

[42]Ibid., pp. 223, 222–29, 234.
[43]Ibid., Part IV: Florida, Louisiana, Texas, pp. 75–76.

kidnapped and taken to Cuba, where slavery was still legal.[44] At South Newport, Georgia, a woman escaped from the plantation of her former master "after much maltreatment." She reported that her former master had "insisted that she and her children were not free, [and] that he cared nothing for 'Lincoln's proclamation.'" When she insisted on leaving "she was confined on bread and water" until she escaped. However, she was forced to leave her children behind.[45]

Howard also reported that at New Altahama, Georgia, army officers had investigated "a case where certain parties were charged with kidnapping colored children and shipping them to Cuba." Two children "mysteriously disappeared" but were then found in Florida after their former owner was placed "under bonds to produce the children." The former owner could not (or would not) explain how the children got to Florida or how he knew where they were.[46] The implication was clear: the former master had kidnapped the children, sent them (or took them) to Florida, and was preparing to send them to Cuba, where they could be sold as slaves.

Understanding the Fourteenth Amendment

It was in the context of this history that the Joint Committee on Reconstruction and Congressman Bingham wrote Section 1 of the Fourteenth Amendment. What did Bingham, Stevens, and their colleagues desire to accomplish with this provision? We can never fully know, of course, but the context of the amendment suggests that their goals were sweeping and broad. Bingham and others in the majority on the Joint Committee understood that they had to protect the life, liberty, safety, freedom, political viability, and property of the former slaves. They had to protect their rights to have meaningful contracts.[47] They had to be able to protect their families in the courtroom and the voting booth, as well as in the marketplace. They had to be protected

---

[44]Ibid., Part III: Georgia, Alabama, Mississippi, Arkansas, p. 33. Howard was the brother of the war hero Major General Oliver Otis Howard, who at this time was the head of Freedmen's Bureau.

[45]Ibid., p. 42.

[46]Ibid., p. 43.

[47]For lawyers, although not necessarily for most historians, this analysis undermined the logic of the early twentieth-century-court's decision in *Lochner v. New York*, 198 U.S. 45 (1905) and was clearly wrong. The idea of "freedom of contract" did not include the right

102 *Paul Finkelman*

from whipping and other forms of cruel and unusual punishment. They desperately needed the protections of the Bill of Rights—fair trials by fair juries, with legal counsel to represent these largely illiterate former slaves. They needed to be able to express themselves in public, which the First Amendment guaranteed them at the federal level, and they need to be protected so they could organize politically. They needed equal schooling to participate in the political process.

It would have been impossible to detail all these needs to explicitly protect them in a constitutional amendment, and thus Bingham did not try. Instead, he used large phrases encompassing grand ideas. He took John Marshall's admonitions in *McCulloch v. Maryland*[48] to heart. He did not try to turn the Constitution into a legal code. Rather, he produced language that would "endure for the ages" and could grow and develop over time. His goal was to reverse the racism and violence of slavery and its immediate aftermath.

At a more basic level, Bingham and the Joint Committee reflected the simple lesson of Major General John W. Turner's testimony. Turner noted that whites in Virginia were "reluctant even to consider and treat the negro as a free man, to let him have his half of the sidewalk or the street crossing."[49] Bingham's goal was to make sure that African Americans, and all other minorities, had full access to their "half of the sidewalk" in the social world, in the political world, in the schools, and in the workplace. It was a radical change to the Constitution and to American notions of federalism. Indeed, by trying to bring those concepts and rights to "all" Americans, their goal was nothing short of a revolution in liberty and justice.

---

to be exploited by powerful employers. That had been the situation in the South before the Fourteenth Amendment. The amendment was designed to prevent this.

[48]17 U.S. (4 Wheat.) 316 (1819).

[49]*Report of the Joint Committee*, Part II: Virginia, North Carolina, South Carolina, p. 4.

Peter Wallenstein

Historicizing the Politics of Reconstruction

Congress and the Fourteenth Amendment, Section 2

Representatives shall be apportioned among the several States according to their respective numbers, counting the whole number of persons in each State, excluding Indians not taxed. But when the right to vote at any election for the choice of electors for President and Vice President of the United States, Representatives in Congress, the Executive and Judicial officers of a State, or the members of the Legislature thereof, is denied to any of the male inhabitants of such State, being twenty-one years of age, and citizens of the United States, or in any way abridged, except for participation in rebellion, or other crime, the basis of representation therein shall be reduced in the proportion which the number of such male citizens shall bear to the whole number of male citizens twenty-one years of age in such State.

Amendment XIV, Section 2

B Y THE END of January 1865, the Thirteenth Amendment had been successfully shepherded through the United States House of Representatives, a struggle depicted in the movie *Lincoln* as told by the director Steven Spielberg.[1] The nation's legislature adjourned a few weeks later— shortly before, as things turned out, the Union army defeated the

---

[1] An early version of this chapter was presented at the U.S. Capitol Historical Society's May 2014 conference under the title "Restoration's Unfinished Business, December 1865: Congress Reconvenes and Addresses the Implications of an End to Slavery."

Confederate military—and did not reconvene until nine months had passed. That is, the second session of the Thirty-Eighth Congress closed shop on March 4, the day of President Abraham Lincoln's second inauguration, and not until December 4 did the first session of the Thirty-Ninth Congress convene. Meanwhile, in early April, Lincoln had been assassinated, just weeks into his second term, and his newly inaugurated vice president, Andrew Johnson, had taken over as president.

Members of Congress, when they met that first week of December 1865, had reason to think, and they were right, that they would soon be hearing that the Thirteenth Amendment had been ratified by enough states to go into the Constitution. By then, therefore, the war had ended, more or less, and slavery was over, also more or less, and it is easy to suppose that this meant that former slaves were now citizens, even citizens with the same political rights as other citizens, and that it would not take a year or two or three after Appomattox to make that happen. There was little reason, however, to assume that any of that would happen, let alone all of it. Historical contingencies occasioned the shape of Reconstruction as it unfolded.

Success in the struggle for Union victory and universal emancipation, whether in Congress or on countless battlefields, led directly to further fights. Members of Congress had to deal with two major implications, neither of them close to resolution, of (1) victory in the war and (2) an end to slavery. On what terms might the states of the recent Confederacy be restored? And who, if not still enslaved, were the former slaves henceforth to be?

Restoration had been an issue ever since South Carolina's leaders voted to secede in December 1860. Victory in the War of the Rebellion that began in 1861 had been struggled toward since the beginning of the conflict. And during the war an end to slavery had emerged not only as a means of Union victory but also as a major war aim. Both objectives—victory *and* abolition—having, it seemed, been reached, Congress had to deal with the actual combination.

Questions surrounding the postslavery condition and rights of black Southerners have long dominated discussions of that era. For scholars in particular, that is the issue that most colors today's sense of the period. But the other concern, not of the *no-longer-slaves* but rather of the *no-longer-Confederate states*, is just as important, and the two issues were tightly tangled up with each other.

Members of Congress asked, and then had to answer, a key question: How could restoration be accomplished safely and effectively? The question was never merely one of restoring representation in Congress, challenging as that turned out to be, but also one of determining how much representation the restored states should have—itself, it is argued here, the central issue in getting the states restored.

So, in the opening weeks of the new Congress, two core considerations occupied lawmakers. One, relating primarily to former slaves and their rights under the law, was subsequently addressed first in the Civil Rights Act of 1866 and then, shortly thereafter, in Section 1 of a proposed Fourteenth Amendment. The other, which related primarily to power in the postwar nation and appeared as Section 2, gets far less notice in the historical literature. That second concern, in no way secondary, remains hidden in plain sight.

Insisting that Section 2 had towering importance to Republican lawmakers at the time does not diminish the historical significance of Section 1, but Section 1 must not get all the attention. The concerns of Americans in the 1860s can scarcely be respected if the concerns of Americans a century and more later, in the present, govern what is noticed about the past. Yet the question of power, more particularly what was to become of matters that had long ago been settled in the 1787 Philadelphia Convention by means of the Three-Fifths Compromise, had at least as much significance to policy makers during the immediate aftermath of the War of the Rebellion.

The postwar position of African Americans had many dimensions. We cannot understand the politics of Reconstruction unless we go back to December 1865 and watch members of Congress wrestle with the many facets of that question. Whatever they thought about racial justice, they worried about political power. The Republic could not be safe, the victory could not be secured, until the basis of representation underwent fundamental renovation.

To sculpt a more realistic representation of the actual history of the years 1865–67 requires that the concerns of Section 2 be brought to the fore—highlighted in historical understanding, viewed in bold relief. To do so is the burden of this chapter. A review of the history of the Three-Fifths Clause through the years before the Civil War can illuminate the situation Congress faced once people who had long been held in slavery no longer counted at three-fifths but rather, no longer slaves, at full value.

Three-Fifths Representation—from 1787 to 1861

Much has been written on the Three-Fifths Clause, a compromise crucial to the success of the 1787 Philadelphia Convention that proposed a new U.S. Constitution for the states to decide whether to ratify.[2] In a census enumeration to be conducted every ten years, slaves would be counted at three-fifths of their actual numbers to determine a state's representation in the House of Representatives. Through the House, the three-fifths formula reached the Electoral College. And through the Electoral College, and its selection of a president, the three-fifths fraction reached the nomination of federal judges. The formula was always central to American national governance.

The three-fifths formula had real consequences, determining which groups of whites would be privileged and which groups disadvantaged. It has often been said that had slaves counted five-fifths in 1796, the Republican Thomas Jefferson from Virginia would have bested the Federalist John Adams of Massachusetts for the presidency that year, and that had it been zero-fifths four years later, Adams would have beat Jefferson in their rematch. Garry Wills wrote a book titled *"Negro President"* to get at the cries of injustice with which northern Federalist whites assailed the legitimacy of Jefferson's election after he won in 1800, thus setting on its long-term course what unfolded as the Virginia Dynasty. New England Federalists complained that "slave representation" had put Thomas Jefferson in the new White House.[3]

The Three-Fifths Clause is a mainstay of some very fine histories of the Early National period, from the Philadelphia Convention of 1787 to the Missouri Crisis of 1819–21. Among books on the politics of slavery in the Early Republic, one by George William Van Cleve admirably retraces developments through those years. He leaps in chronology, however, from the Louisiana Purchase at the end of one chapter to the Missouri Crisis at the start of the next. Regarding the territorial question and its political, social, and economic significance, this narrative strategy makes sense, but it skips the War of 1812 and therefore the Hartford Convention.[4]

---

[2]David Waldstreicher, *Slavery's Constitution: From Revolution to Ratification* (New York, 2009).
[3]Garry Wills, *"Negro President": Jefferson and the Slave Power* (Boston, 2003).
[4]Donald L. Robinson, *Slavery in the Structure of American Politics, 1765–1820* (New York, 1970); Matthew Mason, *Slavery and Politics in the Early American Republic* (Chapel Hill, N.C.,

James Madison, one of Jefferson's fellow Republicans from Virginia, presided at the White House during the War of 1812, a war that had disastrous consequences for the New England area's shipping and other economic activities. Devastation cried out for relief, and in late 1814 several New England states sent delegates to a convention held in Hartford, the state capital of Connecticut, to address the region's severe military and economic problems.

Much the leading study of the subject, James Banner's 1970 book *To the Hartford Convention* offers a brilliant excavation and analysis of Massachusetts state politics in the years leading up to the War of 1812. On the Hartford Convention itself, Banner's findings have largely made their way into textbooks and other general accounts: the "moderates" prevailed, but the convention, in passing some resolutions that addressed their unhappiness at the way the nation was run, proposed alterations in the U.S. Constitution. In speaking briefly of these amendments, Banner notes: "The first and most important provided for the apportionment of representation and direct taxes among the states according to their free white population."[5] After mentioning the proposed zero-fifths formula, the "most important" item, he offers no further discussion of the point.

That very first proposed amendment called for removing the phrase "three-fifths of all other persons" (i.e., slaves) and instead excluding a new group, "all other persons."[6] As for the other proposed amendments, they were significant too. Rather than a simple majority, as for most business, a two-thirds margin would henceforth be required for declarations of war, as well as passage of bills to embargo trade with foreign nations or to admit new states. With Virginia demonstrating an endless train of

---

2006); George William Van Cleve, *A Slaveholders' Union: Slavery, Politics, and the Constitution in the Early American Republic* (Chicago, 2010), pp. 222–25. By no means do all good treatments of the subject place the three-fifths formula near the center of national politics; see Don E. Fehrenbacher, *The Slaveholding Republic: An Account of the United States Government's Relations to Slavery*, completed and edited by Ward M. McAfee (New York, 2001), pp. 40–41, 299 (with no index entry for the Hartford Convention).

[5]James M. Banner Jr., *To the Hartford Convention: The Federalists and the Origins of Party Politics in Massachusetts, 1789–1815* (New York, 1970), pp. 341–43. Banner's language regarding to the contrary, the "free white population" in the proposed new clause said nothing about the race of free people to be included, any more than the original had, only that they not be slaves.

[6]"Amendments to the Constitution Proposed by the Hartford Convention: 1814," http://avalon.law.yale.edu/19th_century/hartconv.asp.

108   *Peter Wallenstein*

candidates—successful candidates—for the presidency, each of whom had been elected to two terms (as opposed to the one non-Virginian, New Englander John Adams, with his single term), future presidents would serve only one term; moreover, no state could supply a winning candidate for two successive terms. If the new Zero-Fifths Clause did not prevent the election of a Virginian, at least he could serve only a single term, and one could not succeed another.[7]

As for whether the "moderates" prevailed at Hartford during that winter of their discontent, here is what they declared about the near future:

> *Resolved,* That if the application of these [New England] States to the government of the United States, recommended in a foregoing Resolution, should be unsuccessful, and peace should not be concluded and the defense of these States should be neglected, as it has been since the commencement of the war, it will in the opinion of this Convention be expedient for the Legislatures of the several [New England] States to appoint Delegates to another Convention, to meet at Boston . . . on the third Thursday of June next [1815] with such powers and instructions as the exigency of a crisis so momentous may require.[8]

Thus the leading study of the Hartford Convention concludes that the moderates controlled it, so the crazies could not take radical action. Yet these demands for changes in the nation's founding document were not to be negotiated; they must be conceded. If they were not agreed to, and the emergency continued, delegates planned to meet again. Consider the analogy. The Hartford Convention was the First Continental Congress, specifying demands and arranging in advance to meet again should those demands be rebuffed. When the First Continental Congress's demands were rejected, a Second Continental Congress met, and in the end it declared independence.[9] Moderates indeed.

The Three-Fifths Clause, then, had been a matter of serious contention at various junctures during the years of the early Republic. At a time of particular crisis, when the stakes seemed so very high in military and economic terms, the Hartford Convention Resolutions capture the intensity of

---

[7]Ibid.

[8]Ibid.

[9]Richard R. Beeman, *Our Lives, Our Fortune and Our Sacred Honor: The Forging of American Independence, 1774–1776* (New York, 2013).

feeling and the degree of importance that could be related to the three-fifths formula.

The issue of perceived unfair overrepresentation of Southern states in national governance persisted over the decades. True, it did not operate alone, nor did it continue to maintain the kind of attention it garnered in the mid-1810s. Another issue, whether Congress could act under the Commerce Clause to terminate the interstate slave trade, surfaced in the 1830s, but then it largely faded. Supplanting both was the issue of the expansion of slavery, tied up as it was with such crucial questions as whether the white/plantation South could continue to dominate on the slavery issue (more than that, on any and all issues in national politics), whether the South could continue to maintain parity in the Senate, whether free white Northerners would have full access to western territories, or whether free Northerners might be pressed into service to seize alleged fugitives from Southern enslavement. For one thing, population growth outside the South outstripped aggregate growth in the slave states such that the Three-Fifths Clause, while continuing to be significant, diminished in salience. Its role as a lightning rod faded somewhat for a generation and more, but it never went away. As William W. Freehling has contextualized the matter through changing times between the Philadelphia Convention and the 1850s, it carried enormous symbolic freight. Moreover, he notes, time and again—from the Missouri Crisis to the Kansas-Nebraska Act—in close votes in Congress it appears to have determined the outcome.[10]

The Three-Fifths Formula in a World without Slaves

Awareness of the three-fifths formula burst forth with renewed force in the immediate aftermath of universal emancipation. Slavery suddenly ended in 1865, and the Three-Fifths Clause surged to the forefront of national politics. James G. Blaine, congressman from Maine, was one of the many people

---

[10]Leonard L. Richards, *The Slave Power: The Free North and Southern Domination, 1780–1860* (Baton Rouge, La., 2000); William W. Freehling, *The Road to Reunion*, vol. 1, *Secessionists at Bay, 1776–1854* (New York, 1990), pp. 146–48, 153–54, 274, 294, 342, 410–11, 559. See also David L. Lightner, *Slavery and the Commerce Power: How the Struggle against the Interstate Slave Trade Led to the Civil War* (New Haven, Conn., 2006); Michael A. Morrison, *Slavery and the American West: The Eclipse of Manifest Destiny and the Coming of the Civil War* (Chapel Hill, N.C., 1997).

110   *Peter Wallenstein*

who abruptly noticed in 1865 a "somewhat startling result" of emancipation.[11] This was the prospect of a surge in representation from the South once the former Confederate states were restored to normal political relations, with members of the House of Representatives elected by the voters, as well as senators by their state legislatures, taking their seats and participating in the making of policy for the nation.

The expansion of slavery, or its abolition, or fugitives from enslavement— such issues vanished with the declaration of an end to slavery. The issue of black representation remained, and it absorbed much of the political energy of the others.

Delegates to the Hartford Convention found themselves up against a dire situation that led them to stipulate conditions for remaining in the Union. By contrast, in December 1865 and through the many months that followed, Congress sought to impose conditions on the secessionist states before they could be safely restored to their former place in the Union.

At the time Congress reconvened in December 1865, what did members know that they could not have known—or had not anticipated—nine months before? What had they been seeing and hearing and writing? They were aware, for one thing, of the new black code that Mississippi had recently enacted for the express purpose of narrowing black Southerners' space to exercise their new freedom, to make real their escape from legal enslavement.[12] Northerners, prominent and obscure, black and white, had been observing early postwar conditions—including journalists who reported back from the South on ominous developments regarding white Unionists in the region as well as former slaves and other black Southerners.[13] Black Southerners themselves were weighing in too.

Manifesto out of Virginia

In mid-1865, at about the time when President Andrew Johnson began opening the door to regularizing governance in the states of the suddenly former

---

[11]Eric Foner, *Reconstruction: America's Unfinished Revolution, 1863–1877* (New York, 1988), p. 252.

[12]William C. Harris, *Presidential Reconstruction in Mississippi* (Baton Rouge, La., 1967), pp. 121–41.

[13]Sidney Andrews, *The South since the War, as Shown by Fourteen Weeks of Travel and Observation in Georgia and the Carolinas* (Boston, 1866).

Confederacy, black Southerners had their own say. For example, meeting in Norfolk, Virginia, in June, three months after Lincoln's second inaugural address and two months after Robert E. Lee surrendered his army at Appomattox, a convention of black Southerners came together.

Styling themselves "citizens," albeit "colored citizens," they addressed their "fellow citizens" on behalf of "the colored population of the southern states generally, and with reference to their claim for equal suffrage in particular." As they crafted their message, one audience they had in mind comprised lawmakers in the nation's capital—no longer Richmond but by that time Washington. The group's leaders included committee chair Thomas Bayne and pastors of two local black churches.[14]

As they assessed their current situation and their expectations and hopes for the future—African Americans' dreams for a world without slavery—they laid claim to the rights and responsibilities of all free people in the world they envisioned. They warned that local white leaders were putting a wide range of the dimensions of black freedom in serious jeopardy. They pointed out that if many freedpeople were dependent on rations from the Freedmen's Bureau, such was only right, for a great many women and children had lost the breadwinner in the family when he fought for the Union and for their freedom. And they warned that many thousands of trained soldiers might have a say in warding off efforts to press them and their families and communities back toward enslavement.[15] Some of those dimensions are the stuff of conventional understanding of the aftermath of war and slavery. Others not so much.

Moreover, mindful of the implications of emancipation for the Three-Fifths Clause, they called on the self-interest of mainstream Northerners in general and members of Congress in particular—what the convention's address to the nation termed "your own interest":

> You have not unreasonably complained of the operation of that clause of the Constitution which has hitherto permitted the slavocracy of the South to wield the political influence which would be represented by a white

---

[14] *Equal Suffrage: Address from the Colored Citizens of Norfolk, Va., to the People of the United States* (1865; reprint ed., Philadelphia, 1969), pp. 1, 8–9; Elizabeth R. Varon, *Appomattox: Victory, Defeat, and Freedom at the End of the Civil War* (Oxford, UK, 2014), pp. 197–98; "Thomas Bayne," https://www.encyclopediavirginia.org/Bayne_Thomas_ca_1824 -1888#start_entry.

[15] *Equal Suffrage*, pp. 3–5, 7.

population equal to three-fifths of the whole negro population; but slavery is now abolished, and henceforth the representation will be in proportion to the enumeration of the whole population of the South, *including people of color,* and it is worth your consideration if it is desirable or politic that the fomenters of this rebellion against the Union, which has been crushed at the expense of so much blood and treasure, should find themselves, after defeat, more powerful than ever, their political influence enhanced by the additional voting power of the other two fifths of the colored population, by which means four Southern votes will balance in the Congressional and Presidential elections at least seven Northern ones.[16]

The Senator and the General

In the North, military and political figures, too, pondered the new exigencies. Senator John Sherman (fig. 1) and his brother, General William Tecumseh Sherman (fig. 2), corresponded throughout the War of the Rebellion and then through the late 1860s. Neither can be confused for radical on the politics of Reconstruction, but both expressed their recognition that at least some policy adjustments had to be made to address the changes that war and abolition had brought to American society and politics. They expressed their concerns even before Congress could return in December 1865 to the nation's business, and then, as Congress navigated through the next few years, they offered their assessments of the changing conditions and the recent past. The core content of both Sections 1 and 2 of the Fourteenth Amendment cropped up again and again.

In May 1865, with Lee's surrender of his army at Appomattox little more than a month past, the senator wrote the general about his apprehensions regarding the coming shape of affairs in the South and the need for a policy. He voiced concerns that provide an illuminating backdrop to both of the first two sections of the Fourteenth Amendment as it emerged many months later. He also pointed to how the two sections of the amendment might relate to each other, as he focused first on black representation in national governance and then on a white monopoly on votes in state lawmaking:

---

[16]Ibid., pp. 4–5 (italics in original).

Fig. 1. Senator John Sherman of Ohio in a ca. 1865–80 photograph. *(Brady-Handy photograph collection, Library of Congress Prints and Photographs Division)*

As to negro suffrage, I admit the negroes are not intelligent enough to vote, but someone must vote their political representation in the State where they live, and their representation is increased by their being free. Who shall exercise this [additional] political power? Shall the rebels do so? If yes, will they not now in effect restore slavery?

Will they not oppress the negroes? Is it not hard to turn these negroes over to the laws made by the very men who endeavored to overthrow the

FIG. 2. General William Tecumseh Sherman in a ca. 1860–90 engraving by J. C. Buttre from a photograph by (E. or H. T.) Anthony. *(Library of Congress Prints and Photographs Division)*

Government? After all, how much more ignorant are these slaves than the uneducated white people down South? I assure you, that while I will not commit myself on these matters, I feel sorely troubled about them, and would be glad to talk with you in respect to them.[17]

There it was, the uncertainty about policy, but the emergent conviction that something would have to be done both about representation in Congress and about the condition and status of former slaves in the South. The end of slavery, though not yet reflected in a ratified Thirteenth Amendment, drove both concerns.

Congress in Session

No sooner than the Congress came back into session in December 1865 did members move swiftly to develop a reconstruction process to counter that of the president. And what became the Fourteenth Amendment's Section 2 proved central to their concerns.

On the very first day, December 4, Representative Thaddeus Stevens of Pennsylvania offered a resolution that a "joint committee of fifteen members" be established to "inquire into the condition of the States which formed the so-called confederate States of America, and report whether they or any of them are entitled to be represented in either House of Congress." The next day, a constitutional amendment was proposed to allocate congressional representation "according to the number of voters in the several States."[18]

The Joint Committee on Reconstruction was soon established, and its work through the months that followed led to the formulation of the Fourteenth Amendment, with its various components, as the main basis for Reconstruction. Meanwhile, Congress moved in early 1866 on a Freedmen's Bureau Bill and a Civil Rights Bill. A proposal in early January resolved

> That, in the opinion of this Committee, the insurgent States cannot, with safety to the rights of all the people of the United States, be allowed to

---

[17]John Sherman to William T. Sherman, May 16, 1865, in Rachel Sherman Thorndike, ed., *The Sherman Letters: Correspondence between General and Senator Sherman from 1837 to 1891* (New York, 1894), p. 251.

[18]*Congressional Globe*, Dec. 4, 5, 1865, 39th Cong., 1st sess., pp. 6, 9.

116   *Peter Wallenstein*

participate in the Government until the basis of representation shall have been modified [what became Section 2], and the rights of all persons amply secured [clearly Section 1, but Section 2 as well], either by new provisions, or the necessary changes of existing provisions, in the Constitution of the United States.[19]

Black men gaining the right to vote could go a long way toward achieving both of these ends, but no agreement in Congress had yet emerged along those lines.

William A. Dunning's classic formulation from 1907, *Reconstruction, Political and Economic, 1865–1877*, observed the problem of representation but did not dwell on it.[20] A few years later, one of his doctoral students focused squarely on it. Georgia native Benjamin B. Kendrick's dissertation in no way celebrated congressional interference in President Johnson's policies, and he was scarcely sympathetic to what animated the Republicans, but he was very clear on their consternation regarding the three-fifths formula: "The particular phase of the negro problem which most concerned Republican politicians in 1865–6 was the problem of representation of the colored population in Congress."[21]

There was never doubt in Congress that the new dispensation, unless fixed in advance of restoration, would inevitably bring enhanced representation for the secessionist states. Kendrick described the majority lawmakers' commitment to preventing any such outcome:

> This state of affairs the Republicans determined to remedy before they would consent to admit the representatives from the rebel states. It is not surprising then to find that the first task undertaken by the committee after its organization was the readjustment of the basis of representation. It was with this subject that the committee busied itself during the first weeks of January, 1866.[22]

Senator William Pitt Fessenden of Maine (fig. 3)—no radical he, but nonetheless a Republican—found himself storm-tossed in the maelstrom of early postwar politics. As was typical of his colleagues, he hoped and

---

[19]Benjamin B. Kendrick, *The Journal of the Joint Committee of Fifteen on Reconstruction: Thirty-Ninth Congress, 1865–1867* (1914; reprint ed., New York, 1969), p. 42.

[20]William Archibald Dunning, *Reconstruction, Political and Economic, 1865–1877* (New York, 1907), pp. 67, 83.

[21]Kendrick, *Journal of the Joint Committee*, p. 198.

[22]Ibid., p. 199.

FIG. 3. Senator William Pitt Fessenden of Maine in a ca. 1860–65 photograph. *(National Archives and Records Administration, Record Group 11)*

118   *Peter Wallenstein*

expected that Congress would be able to work with the new president. In December, when appointed to cochair the Joint Committee on Reconstruction, he still held out the hope and expectation that, as he wrote in a private letter as late as Christmas Eve, 1865, "matters can be satisfactorily arranged—satisfactorily, I mean, to the great bulk of Union men throughout the States."[23] Fessenden continued to expect no major rupture, as would come when the president vetoed the Freedmen's Bureau Bill the following February.

But that was still weeks away. As he said during this earlier time, he was "ready to support [Johnson] to the best of my ability, as every gentleman around me is, in good faith and with kind feeling in all that he may desire that is consistent with my views of duty to the country."[24]

There, of course, was the rub. So, while Republicans ranged widely in their policy desires regarding such matters as black voting and land distribution, the Joint Committee on Reconstruction tried to develop policies that could work and might be widely acceptable in the loyal states even if resisted by leading former Confederates.

Among the many Republicans to voice the need for revisiting the basis of representation, much along the lines of the manifesto from Norfolk back in June, was Roscoe Conkling, representative from New York and a member of the Joint Committee:

> Shall the death of slavery add two-fifths to the entire power which slavery had when slavery was living? Shall one white man have as much share in the government as three other white men merely because he lives where blacks outnumber whites two to one? Shall this inequality exist, and exist only in favor of those who without cause drenched the land with blood and covered it with mourning? Shall such be the reward of those who did the foulest and guiltiest act which crimsons the annals of recorded time? No, sir; not if I can help it.[25]

Writing his brother the senator in February 1866, General Sherman expressed a view that called for as little congressional action as possible, with the great exception that the old Three-Fifths Clause must be renovated:

---

[23]Robert J. Cook, *Civil War Senator: William Pitt Fessenden and the Fight to Save the American Republic* (Baton Rouge, La., 2011), p. 194.

[24]Ibid., p. 193.

[25]Kendrick, *Journal of the Joint Committee*, p. 204.

Historicizing the Politics of Reconstruction 119

I know that the Freedmen Bureau Bill, and that for universal suffrage in the District, are impracticable and impolitic. . . .

I think Mr. Johnson would consent to a modification of the Constitution to change the basis of representation to suit the changed condition of the population [of the] South, but that is all he can or should do.[26]

Congress was moving further than General William Tecumseh Sherman was prepared to go in some matters, but even he signed on in full support of an adjustment in representation.

During the first half of 1866, Congress enacted the Freedmen's Bureau Act and the Civil Rights Act, both of them over vetoes by the president. Beyond such legislation, Congress in general and the Joint Committee in particular pushed ahead in their effort to formulate a Fourteenth Amendment.

The Fourteenth Amendment

As this omnibus measure, reflecting a variety of concerns, took shape, Section 1, designed to place the Civil Rights Act in the Constitution so as to put it beyond subsequent repeal or judicial invalidation, spoke of civil rights and equal protection of the laws. Section 5 empowered Congress to pass additional laws to enforce Section 1.

Section 1 has long been most widely associated with the amendment, but it was hardly alone. Section 4 was designed to guarantee the U.S. national debt that had been taken on to quell the rebellion, to put to rest any uncertainty as to whether state debt contracted in support of the rebellion had any validity, and to end any chance that former slave owners might seek to gain compensation for their losses in that form of property.

Section 2 pointed toward black suffrage but did not mandate it. Rather, Congress continued to defer to the states on the authority to define the electorate, so it offered white Southerners a choice relating voting rights to representation: (1) black men have no vote, but white men do not get to vote black residents' representation (as in the first proposal that, a half century earlier, came out of the Hartford Convention and would have established the fraction as zero-fifths) or (2) black men get the vote, and black men vote

---

[26]William T. Sherman to John Sherman, Feb. 11, 1866, in *Letters*, p. 264.

their own representation, much as the manifesto from Norfolk had argued in mid-1865.

Either way, white men would not get to continue to vote black residents' representation. More to the point, having been defeated in their bid for political independence they would *not* get to come back into the Union with far greater capacity to cause mischief than ever before.

Congressional Republicans might have distinguished between federal elections, on the one hand, and state and local suffrage, on the other. They could, that is, have focused on the need to address the implications of the death of "three-fifths" solely in elections to the U.S. House of Representatives and the presidency. But they did not.

In part, this was because each state legislature appointed the state's U.S. senators, so the state electorate could not be separated in practice from the upper chamber of Congress. In part, too, it was so that black Southerners could protect their own interests as newly freed people and newly denominated citizens. Whatever rights were contemplated in the amendment's Section 1, black Southerners would act as voters to promote their well-being under public policies that they would have some say in shaping. That, too, was important—"moderate" Republicans shared with "radicals" a sense that slavery must be clearly over, that former slaves must be demonstrably free in a world without slavery. Moreover, it seemed imperative that a sufficient constituency be raised that might support loyal/Unionist state governments in the South, and white Unionists had proved too scarce as well as extremely vulnerable. Yet no congressional supermajority was prepared yet to mandate black suffrage.

Running for their political lives in the aftermath of the death of slavery and in the context of a transformed meaning of the Three-Fifths Clause (as well as a politically divided North, thus a potential majority that combined former secessionists with Democrats from loyal states), Republican members of Congress fashioned a collection of demands into what they proposed as the Fourteenth Amendment. This was nonnegotiable. It had to become part of the U.S. Constitution before the states of the recent Confederacy could be safely "restored," their representatives and senators permitted to take their seats. The key component was Section 2.

Seeing the Fourteenth Amendment through to ratification would be a challenge. Not all loyal states, especially such states of the Border South as Maryland and Delaware, could be counted on. Looking to mobilize a

Historicizing the Politics of Reconstruction 121

competing political party to defeat the Republicans in the fall 1866 elections, President Johnson declared political war on the congressional reconstruction program. The white South saw a powerful ally, and many legislators were prepared to take their chances on the outcome. (Contributing, too, to the very widespread Southern white disinclination to accept the terms was a lingering uncertainty as to whether Congress, once the amendment was ratified, might come back with additional demands.)

In early July 1866, looking back at the events of the months after Congress reconvened the previous December, Senator Sherman again wrote his brother. Congress had, he judged,

> adopted no unwise or extreme measures. The Civil Rights Bill and constitutional amendments [by which the senator was referring to the various sections of the Fourteenth] can be defended as reasonable, moderate, and in harmony with Johnson's old position and yours. . . . As to the President, he is becoming Tylerized [a man without a party]. He was elected by the Union party for his openly expressed radical sentiments, and now he seeks to rend to pieces this party. . . . Besides, he is insincere; he has deceived and misled his best friends. I know he led many to believe he would agree to the Civil Rights Bill, and nearly all who conversed with him until within a few days believed he would acquiesce in the amendments, and even aid in securing their adoption.[27]

Hannibal Hamlin, displaced by Andrew Johnson on the Union Party ticket in 1864, would have succeeded to the presidency upon Lincoln's death had he been reelected as vice president. So his approach to the politics of Reconstruction is of more than passing interest. He supported President Johnson as long as he could, but then in the summer of 1866, as Johnson moved to create a rival political party to support his restoration policy in that fall's congressional elections, Hamlin broke with him, with widespread notice.[28]

In his troubled mind, Section 2 seemed entirely at risk. As his grandson recounted a public speech in September by Hamlin back home in Maine:

> He urged the country to stand by Congress and the constitutional amendments. Impartial suffrage without distinction of race or color would have

---

[27] John Sherman to William T. Sherman, July 8, 1866, in *Letters*, p. 276.
[28] Charles Eugene Hamlin, *The Life and Times of Hannibal Hamlin* (Cambridge, Mass., 1899), pp. 507–10.

been the North's wish [this according to the grandson], but if the [former Confederate] States would not accept [black suffrage], the class excluded should not be counted in the basis of congressional representation. "Did we fight down the rebellion to give the [white] South more power?" was the last question Mr. Hamlin asked, and the country pondered it many a year following the madness and folly of Andrew Johnson.[29]

Alone among the former Confederate states, Tennessee ratified the amendment—and saw its members of Congress promptly seated. Then one by one over the coming months, both before and especially after the elections, each of the ten other states turned down the amendment as the basis for Reconstruction.

White Southerners and the Fourteenth Amendment

Not only did the framers in Congress generally see Section 2 as the centerpiece of the Fourteenth Amendment, but their opponents in Southern legislatures did as well. The historian Joseph B. James long ago supplied the pioneering account of "the framing of the Fourteenth Amendment," a focus that the legal historian William E. Nelson later pursued. In a subsequent book, on "the ratification of the Fourteenth Amendment," the historian James E. Bond turned to the next chapter in that story line, as if to ask: What came next? How did the amendment as framed and proposed in 1866 make its way into the Constitution in 1868? In particular, Bond examined the ratification process in the eleven states of the recent Confederacy, with one chapter on each state.[30]

Bond was primarily interested in how the framers of the Fourteenth Amendment—definitely including the Southern men making the decision whether to ratify it—understood the meaning of Section 1, with a nod as well to Section 5, in which Congress would be empowered to act in support of Section 1. What rights did they have in mind when they spoke of citizenship and "equal protection of the laws"? Further out, Bond wished to address

---

[29]Ibid., p. 510.

[30]Joseph B. James, *The Framing of the Fourteenth Amendment* (1939; reprint ed., Urbana, Ill., 1956); William E. Nelson, *The Fourteenth Amendment: From Political Principle to Judicial Doctrine* (Cambridge, Mass., 1988), especially pp. 45–52; James E. Bond, *No Easy Walk to Freedom: Reconstruction and the Ratification of the Fourteenth Amendment* (Westport, Conn., 1997).

Historicizing the Politics of Reconstruction 123

a question regarding the incorporation of the Bill of Rights. Originally framed to contain the authority of the national government, was the Bill of Rights meant henceforth, he asked, through Section 1, to restrain the power of state governments as well?

These are important questions, but on his way to his main interest he observes the following, of far more relevance to the concerns of this chapter:

> The debates [in the South] did not focus primarily on section 1, which today is *the* Fourteenth Amendment. . . . Instead, the debates focused on sections 2 and 3, which dealt respectively with Negro suffrage and apportionment and with the exclusion of rebel leaders from [political] office. While those sections preoccupied [white] Southerners then, today they are "dead letters." . . . In short, the one section which was to become the foundation of so much of modern constitutional law was considered [far] less important than the others—though that fact itself reveals much about the original understanding of its [limited] scope.[31]

On the matter of representation, Bond mentions what he terms the "Southern Compromise Amendment":

> The Southern Compromise Amendment, which some white Southerners proffered in [February] 1867, reinforces the conclusion that they did not [especially] fear recognizing that blacks enjoyed natural rights or granting them civil rights. In fact, the language of Section 3 of that amendment tracks the language of Section 1 of the Fourteenth Amendment. Had the drafters of the Southern Compromise Amendment understood any of those phrases to guarantee political or social rights, they would have balked at including them. As they understood them, however, those phrases were so innocuous that they could be "given away" in exchange for concessions on Sections 2 and 3 of the Fourteenth Amendment, especially if Congress was denied the power to enforce the Section 1 guarantees [certainly if congressional majorities proved disinclined to act] and the definition of their

---

[31]Bond, *No Easy Walk to Freedom*, pp. 8–9. Another close student of the subject offers a variation of this assessment; Michael Perman, *Reunion without Compromise: The South and Reconstruction, 1865–1868* (Cambridge, UK, 1973), pp. 229–47, writes, "Foremost among the objections of the Confederates to the substance of the amendment were the provisions of the third clause" (p. 236). Perman quotes one of those "Confederates" writing to another: "You say we can do without representatives in Congress, but we *must* have a state government" (p. 237).

124   *Peter Wallenstein*

scope was left exclusively to the states [as became largely true within a few years].[32]

Bond concludes, therefore, that—from his tremendous effort to track down and work through the sources necessary to comprehend the process of ratification in each of the secessionist states—the prevailing literature reverses the relative importance in the 1860s, privileging Section 1 (and Section 5) over Section 2 (and Section 3).

If the ten recalcitrant states—or at least enough of them to secure early ratification—had acceded to Section 1 but definitely balked at Section 2, and if Section 2 was even more important than Section 1 to lawmakers in Congress, then Section 2 contributes more than Section 1 to historicizing the Fourteenth Amendment in the politics of early post–Civil War America. Each side saw the aftermath of the old Three-Fifths Clause as a core concern.

Congressional Reconstruction and the Problem of Representation

Two trajectories were bound to collide: insistence in Congress that the amendment be ratified and resistance in the South to complying with that requirement. Congress would not go forward with restoring the ten remaining secessionist states without having first secured the amendment's installation in the Constitution, and those states would not accept terms that required that they choose between black enfranchisement and reduced representation.

---

[32]Bond, *No Easy Walk to Freedom*, pp. 257–58. Bond cites for this alternative amendment a 1950s article by Joseph B. James—which, however, does not use the name Bond adopted and which never reveals the actual language of the document they both reference: "Southern Reaction to the Proposal of the Fourteenth Amendment," *Journal of Southern History* 22 (Nov. 1956):477–97, at pp. 494–96. James in his article (p. 494) characterizes the alternative Fourteenth Amendment as "a compromise proposal as near the original Fourteenth Amendment as Southern sentiment might accept and Northern opposition . . . would permit." The document in its entirety, together with a headnote, "A Southern Proposal for a Fourteenth Amendment," can be found in Walter L. Fleming, ed., *Documentary History of Reconstruction: Political, Military, Social, Religious, Educational, and Industrial, 1865 to the Present*, 2 vols. (Cleveland, Ohio, 1906–7), 1:238–40.

In the immediate aftermath of the fall 1866 congressional elections, in which the Republicans trounced their opposition, the *Repository*, a newspaper published in Franklin County, Pennsylvania, commented on the implications of the Republicans' resounding victory for the ten former Confederate states (all but Tennessee) that had refused to ratify the Fourteenth Amendment. The *Repository* characterized the amendment's provisions as "designed to restore the Union with the least possible inconvenience to the people of the South and the fewest possible restraints consistent with the peace and security of the Government. They were dictated by considerations of mercy as well as expediency."[33]

But those states had rejected the amendment as the basis for restoration, the paper observed in the next weekly edition, and "if the South shall longer persist in her refusal to accept the terms offered, let us take advantage of her refusal, and rebuild the nation's walls on the sure foundation of equal rights."[34]

As one after another among the former Confederate states rejected the Fourteenth Amendment, George William Curtis, editor of *Harper's Weekly*, offered a similar take. In the December 1 issue, he wrote that "the states that remained loyal" through secession and war "are bound to guard the country against any danger that may arise from the unrestricted return of the rebel States, just as they were bound to defend it from the consequences of the attempted secession." And the old three-fifths formula certainly posed such a danger: "Do the Southern Governors mean us to understand—not to put too fine a point upon it—that rebels are humiliated if by their causeless and defeated rebellion they have not gained increased political power?" In view of "the experience of the last five years," what, he wanted to know, might lead people in "the late rebel States . . . to suppose that the loyal people will be turned from their purpose?"[35]

The "terms offered" in the amendment were rejected in those ten states as going too far. As a consequence, Northern terms could and must go further. Section 2 must go into the Constitution. Congress found another means to make that happen.

---

[33] *Franklin Repository*, Nov. 14, 1866, quoted in Edward L. Ayers, *The Thin Light of Freedom: The Civil War and Emancipation in the Heart of America* (New York, 2017), p. 405.

[34] *Repository*, Nov. 21, 1866, quoted in ibid., p. 406.

[35] "The Amendment at the South," *Harper's Weekly*, Dec. 1, 1866.

126 *Peter Wallenstein*

Congressional Reconstruction

In death as in life, then, Southern slavery roiled national politics, and in a manner little recognized in the literature on the era: the political implications, in the immediate post–Civil War period, of the death of slavery, the transformed meaning of the Three-Fifths Clause, and what in turn that might mean for power, politics, and policy in a world that had just left secession, war, and slavery all more or less behind.

Ten of the eleven states of the defeated Confederacy rejected the Fourteenth Amendment, the congressional Republicans' nonnegotiable basis for reunion. They refused to concede that they had to choose between Door Number 1 and Door Number 2.

To get the Fourteenth Amendment ratified, Congress embarked on a major new tactic. In those ten states, new elections would choose delegates to new constitutional conventions. In those elections, black men would vote, and thus black enfranchisement came to much of the South in 1867, something under two years after Congress convened for its first postwar session in December 1865—and more than two years before the Fifteenth Amendment would attempt to settle the matter in another way, for every state.

In fact, large numbers of African Americans, including both former slaves and men formerly in the category of "free persons of color," ran for election as delegates. Many black candidates won, among them Thomas Bayne in Norfolk, Virginia, and thus participated in the process of framing the new constitutions. Regardless of who gained seats as delegates, those constitutional conventions would, Congress required, provide for black suffrage.

And the legislatures elected under those new constitutions, selected to a considerable extent with black votes, would promptly ratify the Fourteenth Amendment as a condition of political restoration. Then perhaps the Republic would be secure. Then the senators chosen by these new state legislatures, and the congressmen elected by the voters in this new expanded electorate, might be permitted to take their seats in Congress. Not until then.

The new formula, as introduced first in the Fourteenth Amendment's Section 2 and then in the March 1867 departure, which led down the path to ratification of all of the Fourteenth Amendment, was designed to result in a vastly different U.S. House of Representatives than would have otherwise materialized. In view of the means employed for securing adoption of the Fourteenth Amendment, with black men voting in state elections, changes in Southern state legislatures might well produce different outcomes in the appointment of U.S. senators. Beyond a shift in outcomes in elections to both houses of Congress as well as the presidency, changes in either or both the presidency and the Senate would alter the selection results for all federal judges.

A Sherman Brothers Retrospective

In November 1867, Senator Sherman wrote the general about Johnson's behavior in the critical year 1866. He expressed certainty that Johnson's rejection of the Fourteenth Amendment had fundamentally altered the course of postwar policymaking:

> The great error of his life was in not acquiescing in and supporting the 14th Amendment of the Constitution in the Thirty-ninth Congress. This he could easily have carried. It referred the suffrage question to each State, and if adopted long ago the whole controversy would have culminated; or if further opposed by the extreme Radicals, they would have been easily beaten. Now I see nothing short of universal suffrage and universal amnesty as the basis.[36]

Both the senator and the general had expressed concern, as early as the spring of 1865, about the degree to which former slaves would be permitted to shed their enslavement. More than that, each had expressed a commitment that something be done about the old Three-Fifths Clause, the basis of representation in the House of Representatives and, through that, the Electoral College. They both recognized the contingent nature of Reconstruction as it unfolded, the probability that had Section 2 provided the actual basis for a postwar regime in 1866, Congress would never have enfranchised black men in March 1867.

Had the secessionist states accepted Section 2, then the carrot-and-stick of enhanced or reduced representation offered in that section might well have influenced white voters and white legislators in each of the former Confederate states as they considered whether to accord black men the right to vote. Whatever they decided would have left the contours of the electorate

---

[36]John Sherman to William T. Sherman, Nov. 1, 1867, in *Letters*, p. 299.

128   *Peter Wallenstein*

in each state up to that state's political actors to determine, whoever they were at any given time. It would have left that decision where it had traditionally been located—but within a very different framework, one that did away with the three-fifths formula as a basic fact of life in American politics and governance.

What If—Lincoln Biographers and the Missing Question

Historians of the Civil War era often ask what Lincoln might have done had he lived to complete his second term, scarcely under way at the time of his assassination, or had he at least lived through the first post-Appomattox year.

One biographer, William C. Harris, notes that a policy of early restoration of the sort that Lincoln had seemed to favor, leaving the matter of determining voting rights in the hands of each state, would necessarily have looked to white Unionists to lead the process in each of the secessionist states. And white Unionists, he observes, came to the postwar world expecting "freedom but not equal rights for blacks"; he says that Lincoln, had he lived, might have managed to "insure, at least for a time, bona fide freedom for blacks," in other words the right, for example, to own land but probably not much, if anything, by way of political rights.[37]

The leading historian of Reconstruction has long been Eric Foner. His book *Reconstruction: America's Unfinished Revolution, 1863–1877*—certainly the dominant account since its publication in 1988—recognizes the three-fifths problem but overall presents the era as a mighty struggle over the postslavery status of black Americans, as primarily, then, a contest over the contours of black freedom.[38]

His prize-winning biography of Lincoln takes a similar approach. Foner goes beyond where Lincoln biographies typically go, but he does not address the Lincoln who would have found himself confronted by abolition's implications for the three-fifths formula. The main question for Foner is how far

---

[37]William C. Harris, *With Charity for All: Lincoln and the Restoration of the Union* (Lexington, Ky., 1997), pp. 265–75, quotes at pp. 268, 275.

[38]Foner, *Reconstruction*, pp. 251–61.

Lincoln would have continued to move in seeking a more robust experience of freedom than simply an end to enslavement.[39]

Both Harris and Foner note Lincoln's ability to change, to grow, and to adjust as conditions changed. Both observe that it is of course impossible to say with certainty what he would have done. Both say, too, though, that they find it inconceivable that he would have let the relations among the president, Congress, and the white South deteriorate to the point that, by late 1866, they clearly had. Both allude to the vote for at least some free men of color in the South, but neither of them argues the centrality of the conundrum that the death of slavery brought to national politics.

Lincoln, it can be hypothesized in view of the quickly emerging issue of the postwar meaning of the Three-Fifths Clause, would nonetheless have come quickly to the realization that so many Republican members of Congress did. The kinder, gentler Lincoln might well have proved indistinguishable on this issue from the members of Congress who came to be seen as the radicals on black suffrage. It seems very probable that he would have joined the Republican consensus that there had to be—as Thomas Bayne, Senator Sherman, Representative Conkling, and so many others saw as imperative—a fundamental alteration in the three-fifths formula. Most Republicans of necessity, given the circumstances they came to see about the formula for congressional representation, had to be "radicals." The adjective in that context appears redundant.

In a brief treatment, *Lincoln and Reconstruction*, the historian John C. Rodrigue includes "determining representation in Congress with elimination of the 'three-fifths' clause" among the range of issues that Lincoln would have faced had he lived. By no means does Rodrigue wish to downplay "the importance of Lincoln's racial thought and its implications for postwar reconciliation," but he observes that perhaps historians' "traditional focus" on such matters is a bit "misplaced."

Rodrigue does not return to the three-fifths problem but rather moves to a consideration of black laborers' widespread landlessness in the postwar world.[40] Yet he opens up space for an interpretation that something like the Fourteenth Amendment, with Section 2 as well as Section 1—and the

---

[39]Eric Foner, *The Fiery Trial: Abraham Lincoln and American Slavery* (New York, 2010), pp. 330–36.

[40]John C. Rodrigue, *Lincoln and Reconstruction* (Carbondale, Ill., 2013), pp. 144–45.

130 *Peter Wallenstein*

congressional insistence on its ratification as a nonnegotiable condition of political restoration—was perhaps (whatever the details) virtually inevitable.

Then again, had enough former Confederate states ratified the Fourteenth Amendment as it took final shape in 1866, black suffrage in those states might well not have come at all in the postwar years—or not as fully as it did, nor when it did.

Perspectives from the 1860s—and from the Present

Historians commonly misperceive the most important section of Congress's handiwork in the Fourteenth Amendment, it is argued here, or rather confuse what became the most important part in the middle third of the twentieth century with what was, for perhaps far more whites in America, North and South, the most important in 1865–67, when Congress began pondering what to do in the aftermath of an end to enslavement and then proposed the amendment and sent it to the states, looking to gain approval.[41] When most Southern states rejected it, too many to permit its ratification (if, that is, the seceded states were included in the number, three-fourths of which had to ratify the amendment for it to go into effect), Congress had to arrange some other means to get the amendment into the Constitution. The result is known as Congressional Reconstruction, or sometimes Radical Reconstruction, which was finally embarked on in March 1867, the first attempt at securing the Fourteenth Amendment having been rebuffed by most of the secessionist states.

Thus the key to the politics of Reconstruction, hidden in plain sight, gets bypassed. Summing up the conventional understanding, a recent book-length survey of the era of the Civil War and Reconstruction tarries enough

---

[41]A statement of this thesis of the centrality of the three-fifths problem, generally bypassed or understated in subsequent literature, appeared in J. G. Randall and David Donald, *The Civil War and Reconstruction* (1961; second ed., rev. with enlarged bibliography, Lexington, Mass., 1969), pp. 580–86. For another such treatment of the Three-Fifths Clause, see W. R. Brock, *American Crisis: Congress and Reconstruction, 1865–1867* (New York, 1963), especially pp. 21–23. Garrett Epps supplies a sustained approach along these lines in *Democracy Reborn: The Fourteenth Amendment and the Fight for Equal Rights in Post–Civil War America* (New York, 2006). See also Xi Wang, *The Trial of Democracy: Black Suffrage and Northern Republicans, 1860–1910* (Athens, Ga., 1997), pp. 14–28, and Mark Wahlgren Summers, *The Ordeal of the Reunion: A New History of Reconstruction* (New York, 2014), pp. 3–4, 90–104.

at the Fourteenth Amendment to point out Sections 1 and 3. Section 1, declaring that no state could "deprive any person of life, liberty, or property, without due process of [law]," is clearly of central interest to the authors of that book, so one must understand in that context their entire discussion of the politics of Reconstruction. As for Section 3, it "barred some prominent former Confederates from holding high [as well as lower] political positions," at least "until the region stabilized enough to support a genuine two-party system."[42] (But that "genuine two-party system" would evidently emerge with an all-white electorate, since any provision for, let alone a constitutional guarantee of, black suffrage in the South had yet to enter the picture before 1867.)

So, the postwar black codes that, one after another, all-white legislatures enacted in the former Confederate states, together with such large-scale white-on-black violence as occurred in 1866 in Memphis and New Orleans, were what "united moderate and radical Republicans." The authors are consistent in this single-minded focus on "the basic civil rights of the freed people" as the chief (if not sole) concern among Republican lawmakers in Congress as well as among mainstream white Northerners. The Civil Rights Act of 1866, vetoed by President Johnson and then enacted over his veto, reflected an urgent response to these challenges to Republicans' demands. So far, so good. But in turn, apprehension as to "the president's possible sabotage of the Civil Rights Act," according to this understanding, sufficiently explains what "led Republicans to propose the Fourteenth Amendment."[43]

In this view, the Fourteenth Amendment appears, and properly so, central to the politics of Reconstruction, yet the implicit understanding is that Section 1 was what was at stake, since Section 2 never gets noticed. "Tennessee had been readmitted to the Union after ratifying the Fourteenth Amendment in July 1866," the authors write, and was therefore already restored and thus exempted when Congressional Reconstruction came along in March 1867. After new constitutional conventions (elected this time by biracial electorates) worked up acceptable new state constitutions for the ten remaining former Confederate states during the months to follow, and after

---

[42]Gary W. Gallagher and Joan Waugh, *The American War: A History of the Civil War Era* (State College, Penn., 2015), p. 205.
[43]Ibid., pp. 200–206.

132   *Peter Wallenstein*

new legislatures had been elected under those instruments, "the last step was ratifying the Fourteenth Amendment."[44] At that point, members of Congress would be admitted from those ten states, and Reconstruction would be complete, the Union restored, and the *fruits of abolition* secured.

With ratification of the Fourteenth Amendment, the "basic civil rights of the freedpeople" would be protected under the Constitution, far more surely than they had been with the 1866 Civil Rights Act, let alone before that. But this view bypasses Republicans' insistence that the *fruits of victory* also be secured, the Republic safe from subversion in a hostile takeover, whether the security required by Republicans came with black suffrage neutralizing much of the electoral power of white supremacists or with reduced representation reflecting a continuation of black disfranchisement.

The End of Three-Fifths in American Political Life

The congressional framers of the Fourteenth Amendment knew they *wanted* the gist of what became both Sections 1 and 2. They knew they *had* to have Section 2. Centering Section 2 can make sense of the riddle of Reconstruction, better identifying the core issue in the politics of those first postwar years.

That Section 2 goes relatively unconsidered in the literature on Reconstruction has several possible explanations. The Dunning historians of the early twentieth century were not looking for reasons the Republicans might have been legitimately concerned about their survival as a party and all it stood for. (Benjamin B. Kendrick stands out as the great exception, as he sought to understand the Joint Committee on Reconstruction, created by Congress in December 1865.) Then came the civil rights lawyers who, during the middle third of the twentieth century, litigated against racial disparity as matters of constitutional law concerning state action and equal protection of the laws. In their wake, a new generation of scholars focused on Section 1 as the key to Reconstruction—as the key to the "first" Reconstruction as well as to the "second" Reconstruction.[45]

---

[44]Ibid., p. 206.
[45]For an able review of the main currents of Reconstruction historiography, see Michael Perman, "The Politics of Reconstruction," in Lacy K. Ford, ed., *A Companion to*

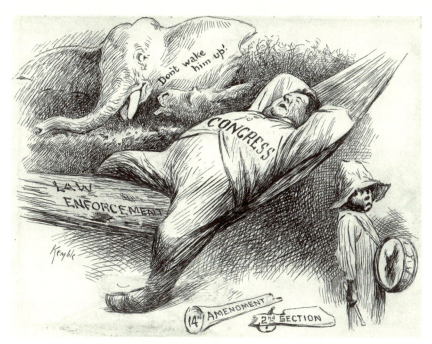

FIG. 4. A political cartoon by E. W. Kemble in 1902 satirized the lack of congressional enforcement of the second section of the Fourteenth Amendment, depicted as a broken blunderbuss at the feet of Congress as a sleeping fat man. *(Library of Congress Prints and Photographs Division)*

Subterranean developments are by their nature not particularly visible, even if they fundamentally alter the landscape. Even scholars who acknowledge the problem of representation typically move on as if it requires no further consideration in tracking the politics of Reconstruction.

The deliberations that led to both Section 1 and Section 2, the need to amend the Constitution, the sense of urgency that the amendment be ratified before restoration of the secessionist states, all these had their beginnings as soon as Congress met in December 1865. The combination of victory and abolition, in the context of the old Three-Fifths Clause, mandated close attention to what became the Fourteenth Amendment's Section 2 as well as what became Section 1.

---

the Civil War and Reconstruction (Malden, Mass., 2005), pp. 323–41. Notably missing, however, is an emphasis on Section 2.

The Fourteenth Amendment was simply central to the congressional politics of the early post–Civil War years. True, by the end of the nineteenth century and for well into the twentieth, Section 1 proved pretty ineffective; but it supplied the constitutional basis for the civil rights struggle of the 1950s and 1960s. Section 2 also faded in significance (fig. 4), even more so, as the threat of reduced representation was never implemented, despite widespread black disfranchisement over much the same period; and leaders of the one-party former Confederacy were able to thwart congressional legislation in support of civil rights until even later than when federal courts began acting to revive the promises of Reconstruction. For the Thirty-Ninth Congress, however, Section 2 stood even taller than Section 1.

Well before the Black Codes of 1865–66, or the tussle in 1866 between President Johnson and Congress over the Freedmen's Bureau Bill and the Civil Rights Act, or the white-on-black violence that made headlines that year, the emphasis on what became Section 2 can be seen in such declarations from mid-1865 as the black manifesto from Norfolk and the correspondence between the Sherman brothers.

Political tensions over black representation recurred under slavery and returned with emancipation—reverberated from 1787 to 1815 and reached a new crescendo in 1865–67. By the time of that last crisis, one response to the issue of who, if anyone, would vote African Americans' representation went in a novel direction. Under the Resolution of 1867 they would vote it themselves. For a time, at least, it was so.

William E. Nelson

Sectionalism, the Fourteenth Amendment, and the End of Popular Constitutionalism

STUDENTS OF AMERICAN legal history have recently developed a significant interest in popular constitutionalism—the concept that the people themselves rather than judges should determine the substance and meaning of the constitution. Historians have convincingly shown that from the 1760s, when major issues first arose about the power of Parliament to tax and regulate the colonies, to the end of the eighteenth century, the people debated publicly what their constitution meant and resolved differences mainly through popular, sometimes even violent, action. Events such as the Boston Tea Party—indeed, the War of Independence itself—come to mind. Judicial decision making played only a minor role in constitutional debate.[1]

According to twenty-first-century law, in contrast, the people have little power over the constitution; judges determine what it means. Since *Cooper*

This chapter was delivered in nearly its present form in May 2015 as the keynote address at the annual symposium of the U.S. Capitol Historical Society. My thanks to Paul Finkelman and the society for inviting me to speak. At that time, the chapter was an early draft of what now appears as chapter 9 of William E. Nelson, *The Common Law in Colonial America*, vol. 4, *Law and the Constitution on the Eve of Independence, 1735–1776* (New York, 2017). As readers of this chapter and the book will plainly see, my views changed substantially as I continued during the interim to think about the matters discussed herein.

[1]See, e.g., Larry Kramer, *The People Themselves: Popular Constitutionalism and Judicial Review* (New York, 2004); John Phillip Reid, *Constitutional History of the American Revolution*, 4 vols. (Madison, Wis., 1986–93); William E. Nelson, *The Common Law in Colonial America*, vol. 4, *Law on the Eve of Revolution, 1730–1775* (New York, 2017).

135

136   *William E. Nelson*

v. Aaron in 1958,[2] the Supreme Court of the United States has claimed final, dispositive authority over constitutional interpretation; it has repeatedly asserted "the basic principle that the federal judiciary is supreme in the exposition of the law of the Constitution."[3] When and how did this change occur?

The core claim of this chapter is that the change occurred when it became impossible in the mid-nineteenth century to envision the American people as a cohesive political entity. Instead, the nation had become divided into majority and minority factions, which then sought to use the written constitution of 1787, as originally drafted and ratified by the Founding Fathers, in support of their interests and to prohibit emerging majorities from acting contrary to those interests.

Let me begin with the eighteenth century, whose popular constitutionalism rested first and foremost on the fact that the people were interpreting a customary constitution rather than a formally enacted document. The constitution was not a set of written commands issued by an authoritative body informing government officials of the scope and limits of their power. Of course, there were some writings, such as Magna Carta, the Declaration of Rights, and the Act of Settlement, that were part of the constitution, but the reason for their inclusion was not their enactment by the king or Parliament. They were part of the constitution because the people had come to accept them as such.

The eighteenth-century English constitution consisted of those fundamental norms and practices, some in writing but some not, to which the English people as a whole had consented and by which they had come over time to be governed. Of course, perfect agreement did not exist as to the specific content of those norms and practices. Some individuals were always challenging whatever tentative and fleeting consensus most other people had accepted. Thus, the eighteenth-century constitution did not consist of readily identifiable, fixed rules; ultimately, the constitution, in the notable language of John Phillip Reid, was "whatever could be plausibly argued and forcibly maintained."[4]

---

[2]358 U.S. 1 (1958).
[3]Ibid., p. 18.
[4]John Phillip Reid, "In a Defensive Rage: The Uses of the Mob, the Justification in Law, and the Coming of the American Revolution," *New York University Law Review* 49 (1974):1043, 1087.

The imprecision of the constitution gave it great flexibility over time. The English constitution of 1760 was not the same as the constitution of 1690, let alone that of 1630. It had evolved. Parliamentary legislation had contributed to the evolution, but the evolutionary process did not consist solely of constitutive acts. Indeed, some acts, such as Oliver Cromwell's Instrument of Government, had come to possess no force at all. What made the constitution evolve was the gradual, sometimes imperceptible changes in the public's understanding of the norms and practices that composed the foundation on which government rested.

The document drafted in 1787 and ratified in 1788 that we now view as *the* Constitution of the United States—that is, as the entire American constitution—was not, I urge, so understood by the people of 1787–88. Rather, it was simply part of a still largely customary American constitution. I disagree with Jefferson Powell's claim that the great "innovation" of the Revolutionary era "was to identify 'the Constitution' with a single normative document instead of a historical tradition"—as a written superior law set above the entire government against which all other law and all government action is to be measured.[5]

I do not deny that some Americans in the late 1760s began to argue that "the fundamental Pillars of the Constitution should be comprised in one act or instrument" so that "not a single point may be subject to the least ambiguity." They urged that it was necessary to limit government "by some certain terms of agreement" that would provide security against "the danger of an indefinite dependence upon an undetermined power." By 1776, the idea that "all constitutions should be contained in some written Charter" surely was in the air.[6]

But older concepts of a customary constitution and popular constitutionalism also persisted. James Otis Jr. had argued as early as 1761 that "an act against natural equity is void" and that the people and even the courts should "pass such acts into disuse."[7] Many Americans afterward continued to believe that all law must be consistent with higher law and natural equity and

---

[5]H. Jefferson Powell, "The Original Understanding of Original Intent," *Harvard Law Review* 98 (1985):885, 902. See also Gordon S. Wood, *The Creation of the American Republic, 1776–1787* (Chapel Hill, N.C., 1969), p. 260.

[6]Quoted in Wood, *Creation of the American Republic,* pp. 267, 268.

[7]John Adams's Report of the First Argument in February 1761 in *Paxton's Case,* Quincy 469, 474 (Mass. Super. Ct. 1761).

138 *William E. Nelson*

should be held null, void, and of no effect if it was not. Thus, for John Dickinson, rights were

> not annexed to us by parchments and seals. They [were] created in us by the decrees of Providence, which establish the laws of our nature. They [were] born with us; exist with us; and cannot be taken from us by any human power, without taking our lives. In short, they are founded on the immutable maxims of reason and justice.

Philip Livingston was another who, before the Declaration of Independence, agreed that people were entitled to their rights "by the eternal laws of right reason."[8]

The coming of independence changed nothing. Eleven states drafted written constitutions between 1776 and 1780 to fill in gaps in their customary constitutions created when British authority was expelled from the colonies. But these written constitutions, it was argued, needed to adhere "to the ancient habits and customs of the people . . . in the distribution of the supreme power of the state." As state legislatures went into operation under their written constitutions, critics continued to assert that even if statutes were consistent with some constitutional text, those that "militate[d] with the fundamental laws, or impugn[ed] the principles of the constitution, [were] to be judicially set aside as void, and of no effect." It continued to be said that all law "must be restrained within the bounds of *reason, justice*, and *natural equity*."[9]

Clearest of all in criticizing written constitutions was a series of articles by Noah Webster in 1787–88. Webster wrote that "liberty is never secured by such paper declarations; nor lost for want of them." According to Webster, government

> takes its form and structure from the genius and habits of the people; and if on paper a form is not accommodated to those habits, it will assume a new form, in spite of all the formal sanctions of the supreme authority of a State. . . . Unless the advocates for unalterable constitutions of government, can prevent all changes in the wants, the inclinations, the habits and the circumstances of the people, they will find it difficult, even with all their declarations of unalterable rights, to prevent changes in government. A

---

[8]Quoted in Wood, *Creation of the American Republic*, pp. 293, 294.
[9]Quoted in ibid., pp. 431, 456 (emphasis in original).

The End of Popular Constitutionalism 139

paper-declaration is a very feeble barrier against the force of national habits, and inclinations.[10]

The nation's first decade of experience under the federal constitution in many ways proved Webster right; think, for example, how quickly the actual procedures for electing the president became radically different from what the framers had put down on paper.

Lawyers and judges similarly continued to have recourse to higher law norms outside written constitutions well into the nineteenth century. For instance, in the decade after Webster's articles, when the Georgia legislature repealed an act under which a vast tract of land in Mississippi had been sold, investors in New England who had bought some of the land sought an opinion from Alexander Hamilton, who was then in private practice, about the legitimacy of the repeal act. Hamilton responded that it was "a contravention of the first principles of natural justice . . . to revoke a grant of property regularly made for valuable consideration, under legislative authority."[11] Congressman Robert Goodloe Harper similarly argued that the Georgia land sales were contracts and that it was "an invariable maxim of law, and of natural justice, that one of the parties to a contract, cannot by his own act, exempt himself, from its obligation." After the Georgia repeal had become a significant national political issue, Jedidiah Morse gave wide publicity to the Hamilton-Harper view in his *American Gazetteer*, where he wrote that "it was generally agreed by the informed part of the community, that . . . the [Georgia] repealing law must be considered as a 'contravention of the first principles of natural justice . . .' and void."[12]

When the Georgia repeal act came before the Supreme Court in 1810 in *Fletcher v. Peck*,[13] Chief Justice John Marshall relied in part on the written constitution's contract clause. But he also invalidated the act on the ground of "general principles which are common to our free institutions," which "prescribe some limits to the legislative power," among them that "the property of an individual, fairly and honestly acquired," could not "be seized

---

[10]Quoted in ibid., p. 377.

[11]Alexander Hamilton's Opinion on the Georgia Repeal Act, in C. Peter Magrath, *Yazoo: Law and Politics in the New Republic; The Case of* Fletcher v. Peck (Providence, R.I., 1966), pp. 149, 150.

[12]Quoted in ibid., pp. 20, 23.

[13]10 U.S. (6 Cranch) 87 (1810).

140 William E. Nelson

without compensation."[14] In his concurring opinion, Justice William John-son relied only on "general principle, on the reason and nature of things, a principle that will impose laws even on the Deity."[15]

Other cases similarly invalidated legislation on the basis of general princi-ples of natural justice and equity rather than written constitutional text.[16] *McCulloch v. Maryland*,[17] in turn, revealed another aspect of popular consti-tutionalism and the customary constitution. The case, involving the consti-tutionality of the Second Bank of the United States, was about the power of Congress under the constitution of 1787, not about the application of funda-mental, higher law norms antecedent to that written constitution. Nonethe-less, Chief Justice Marshall did not resolve the case by turning only to an analysis of the written text or to a discussion of what those who had drafted and ratified the text intended when they used the language they chose. He also examined the meaning that had been given to the constitution since its adoption. He noted that even when Congress first established a bank, the question of its constitutionality was never concealed from "an un-suspecting legislature, and pass[ed] unobserved." From the outset, the argu-ments in favor of the bank were "completely understood, and [were] opposed with equal zeal and ability." After consideration "first in the fair and open field of debate, and afterwards in the executive cabinet," the bank opened. Although the charter of the First Bank was not renewed, "a short experi-ence of the embarrassments to which the refusal to revive it exposed the government, convinced [even] those who were most prejudiced against the measure of its necessity." Marshall therefore concluded that such "an expo-sition of the constitution, deliberately established by legislative acts, on the faith of which" people had advanced "immense property," could not "be lightly disregarded."[18]

As late as the 1860s, even the people themselves did not always consider the document of 1787–88, frozen in time, as the entirety of America's con-stitution. They paid heed to other norms and practices beyond the 1787 text. Consider the abolitionists. One leading abolitionist, Lysander Spooner, for

---

[14]10 U.S. (6 Cranch) at 135.
[15]10 U.S. (6 Cranch) at 139, 143 (concurring opinion).
[16]See *Calder v. Bull*, 3 U.S. (3 Dallas) 386 (1798); *Terrett v. Taylor*, 13 U.S. (9 Cranch) 43 (1815); *Wilkinson v. Leland*, 27 U.S. (2 Pet.) 627 (1829); *Gardner v. Village of Newburgh*, 2 Johns. Ch. 162 (N.Y. Chancery Ct. 1816).
[17]17 U.S. (4 Wheat.) 316 (1819).
[18]17 U.S. (4 Wheat.) at 401–2.

example, adopted a common position that the Declaration of Independence, with its aspirational language about the equality of all men and their entitlement to liberty, was "the constitutional law of this country for certain purposes"; he continued that slavery was "so entirely contrary to natural right; so entirely destitute of authority from natural law; . . . that nothing but express and explicit provision can be recognized, in law, as giving it any authority."[19] Some two decades later, a Lincoln supporter named Grosvenor Lowrey called the written constitution "not the *cause*, but the *means* of American freedom." Thus, whenever the constitution was "the subject of consideration," it was necessary, according to Lowrey, to look beyond and "through the Constitution to that broader charter on which it rests [—] . . . a higher law which shall sustain and be in agreement with it."[20]

In sum, the customary constitution and popular constitutionalism remained vibrant and effectual into the era of the Civil War. The people, along with judges and political leaders, continued to play a significant role in determining the constitution's substance and meaning. In doing so, they scrutinized the text of not only the 1787–88 document but also other documents, especially the Declaration of Independence, as well as unwritten doctrines of higher, fundamental law. Finally, the customary constitution— that which could be plausibly argued in a fashion convincing to large numbers—retained enormous capacity for change: both the antislavery constitutionalism around which the Republican Party coalesced in the late 1850s and the secessionist constitutionalism of the South that had scarcely existed thirty years earlier.

Nonetheless, as slavery became an increasingly divisive issue in American life in the years after 1830, change began to occur in how judges and political leaders thought about the constitution. It had made sense into the 1820s, when the United States still possessed a comparatively cohesive political order, to think of the people as an entity and of the constitution as a set of customary practices which that entity collectively could change over time. But once the nation became divided into sections—a majority antislavery section and a minority proslavery section—the constitution's

---

[19]Lysander Spooner, *The Unconstitutionality of Slavery* (Boston, 1845), pp. 39, 43–44.
[20]Grosvenor P. Lowrey, *The Commander-in-Chief: A Defense upon Legal Grounds of the Proclamation of Emancipation; and an Answer to Ex-Judge Curtis' Pamphlet, Entitled "Executive Power,"* 2nd ed. (New York, 1863), in Frank Freidel, ed., *Union Pamphlets of the Civil War, 1861–1865* (Cambridge, Mass., 1967), 1:474, 480–81.

142   *William E. Nelson*

capacity for collective change vanished; instead, different groups in the slavery debate sought to show how the written constitution of 1787, as originally drafted and ratified by the Founding Fathers, supported their interests. In particular, the South argued and the Supreme Court agreed that the original constitution embraced a binding bargain that protected slavery from antislavery ideas that were developing in the North.

Prigg v. Pennsylvania,[21] which relied on the Constitution's fugitive slave clause to invalidate a Pennsylvania anti-kidnapping statute, was an early manifestation of the changing modes of thought. In his opinion for the court, Justice Joseph Story wrote that

> it is well known, that the object of this clause was to secure to the citizens of the slave-holding states the complete right and title of ownership in their slaves, as property, in every state in the Union into which they might escape from the state where they were held in servitude. The full recognition of this right and title was indispensable to the security of this species of property in all the slave-holding states; and, indeed, was so vital to the preservation of their domestic interests and institutions, that it cannot be doubted, that it constituted a fundamental article, without the adoption of which the Union could not have been formed. Its true design was to guard against the doctrines and principles prevalent in the non-slave-holding states, by preventing them from intermeddling with, or obstructing, or abolishing the rights of the owners of slaves.[22]

Note how this originalist analysis by Justice Story differed sharply in its approach from the popular constitutionalist analysis with which Chief Justice Marshall had begun *McCulloch v. Maryland*.

Similar recourse to originalist analysis occurred again in Chief Justice Roger Taney's opinion in *Scott v. Sandford*.[23] Taney, who, like Story, was concerned with protecting the South from the growing antislavery populism of the North, wrote that the court could not

> give to the words of the Constitution a more liberal construction . . . than they were intended to bear when the instrument was framed and adopted. Such an argument would be altogether inadmissible in any tribunal called on to interpret it. If any of its provisions are deemed unjust, there is a mode

---

[21] 41 U.S. (16 Pet.) 539 (1842).
[22] 41 U.S. (16 Pet.) at 611.
[23] 60 U.S. (19 How.) 393 (1857).

The End of Popular Constitutionalism 143

prescribed in the instrument itself by which it may be amended; but while it remains unaltered, it must be construed now as it was understood at the time of its adoption. . . . [A]s long as it continues to exist in its present form, it speaks not only in the same words, but with the same meaning and intent with which it spoke when it came from the hands of its framers, and was voted on and adopted by the people of the United States. Any other rule of construction would abrogate the judicial character of this court.[24]

The Civil War, which broke out four years later, saved the Union, but it did not bring an end to sectionalism on issues of race. The idea of a cohesive body politic that could transform the constitution over time remained a mirage. One result was that the constitution increasingly came to be seen as a body of fixed, politically enacted rules rather than an accumulation of flexible, customary, popular norms.

In particular, the Unionists who won the Civil War and controlled Congress in its aftermath, like antebellum Southerners whose views had been reflected in *Prigg* and *Dred Scott*, came to understand the constitution as a mechanism for the permanent codification of their values in the event a time should come when a majority of the American people no longer shared them. Those Unionists used the Reconstruction amendments, especially the Fourteenth, for that end. In short, "the Fourteenth Amendment was understood" not as a constitutional provision subject to future popular interpretation but "as a peace treaty to be administered by Congress in order to secure the fruits of the North's victory in the Civil War."[25] The Union army had suffered 364,511 deaths in the war—more than one out of every fifty men who lived in the North.[26] Northerners understood that it would "take a good deal of whitewash to cover the blood that ha[d] been shed."[27] "[T]he loyal sentiment of the Country" demanded that the "brave boys who offered their lives upon the Altar of their country" not be "sacrificed . . . in vain."[28] Thus, the goal of the Reconstruction amendments in general, and of the Fourteenth Amendment in particular, was to establish "a permanent

---

[24]60 U.S. (19 How.) at 426.

[25]William E. Nelson, *The Fourteenth Amendment: From Political Principle to Judicial Doctrine* (Cambridge, Mass, 1988), pp. 110–11.

[26]Ibid., p. 46.

[27]John W. Pease to John Sherman, Mar. 14, 1866, in John Sherman Papers, Library of Congress (LC), Washington, D.C.

[28]W. Bryce to John Sherman, Jan. 21, 1866, in Sherman Papers, LC.

144 *William E. Nelson*

peace"[29] "to the end that the curse of civil war may never be visited upon us again."[30] The goal was "to secure in a . . . permanent form the dear bought victories achieved in the mighty conflict,"[31] in the words of a June 1866 resolution of the Union Party of Ohio, "upon such stable foundations that rebellion and secession will never again endanger our National existence."[32]

Such an understanding of the Fourteenth Amendment, not as one of many norms and practices contributing to the nation's future constitution but as a stable foundation anchoring that constitution, transformed American constitutionalism. Now that Unionists had adopted the antebellum, pro-Southern originalism of *Prigg* and *Dred Scott*, no significant interest group viewed the constitution as a body of custom that could evolve over time. Instead, the constitution became a permanent command put in place by wartime victors who demanded security for the fruits of their victory. Determining the meaning of the constitution thus no longer authorized those who would be affected by its meaning to decide what they wanted it to mean. Instead, the meaning of the constitution was set in stone by those who had drafted and ratified it. The people who had to live under the constitution no longer had a role to play in deciding what it meant. The constitution's meaning instead had to be parsed by experts—lawyers in the role of forensic historians—who could look back into the past to intuit what the drafters and ratifiers had intended. Popular constitutionalism was gone; originalism had replaced it.

Of course, this overstates both the suddenness and the thoroughness of the shift from a customary to an originalist constitution. As just seen above, originalism emerged before the Civil War, and the idea of the constitution as custom has persisted, as exemplified by Justice John Marshall Harlan II's mid-twentieth-century dissent in *Poe v. Ullman*,[33] where the justice supported his decision on the ground of "those rights 'which are . . . *fundamental*; which belong . . . to the citizens of all free governments'"—rights extracted from a "tradition [that] is a living thing"—that is, from "the traditions from

---

[29]Samuel Craig to Thaddeus Stevens, Feb. 5, 1866, in Thaddeus Stevens Papers, Library of Congress, Washington, D.C.

[30]*Congressional Globe*, Mar. 19, 1864, 38th Cong., 1st Sess., p. 1203 (remarks of Rep. James F. Wilson [R-IA]).

[31]"Governor's Message," *Iowa State Register* (Des Moines), Jan. 15, 1868, p. 3, col. 7.

[32]Resolutions of June 19, 1866, in Sherman Papers, LC.

[33]367 U.S. 497, 522 (1961).

which . . . [the nation] developed as well as the traditions from which it broke."[34]

I am guilty of overstatement, however, for a good reason—to make a central analytical point. If one conceives of constitutional provisions as fundamental but flexible norms and practices by which a cohesive, democratic community governs itself at any given moment in time, then the people of the community at that moment in time possess collective power to determine what those constitutional provisions mean, and a court charged with deciding a case should look to the people of the moment for guidance. If, by contrast, one conceives of constitutional provisions as codifications of past political or military victories designed to assure the victors that even if they lose power and become a minority their victories will be preserved in the future, then experts of some sort are needed to determine exactly what the past codified, and a court charged with deciding a case should look to experts for guidance, not to ordinary people.

The Fourteenth Amendment can be understood both as a flexible, foundational norm and as a permanent guarantee designed to secure in all times the rights even of minorities. The Supreme Court has tended to understand it mainly as the latter. Let me end by offering two reasons why the amendment can be understood in both ways, as well as why I think the court has understood it mainly as a permanent guarantee protecting minorities.

The first reason for the amendment's flexibility is the language the drafters used in Section 1. The drafters may have wanted the Fourteenth Amendment to serve the future as a stable anchor of the peace they understood the Civil War had won. But they could not agree among themselves on the specific terms of that peace. In particular, they could not agree whether to extend the right to vote to freedmen. So they papered over their disagreement with vague language—privileges and immunities, due process, and equal protection—that the Supreme Court, the institution eventually charged with enforcing the drafters' anchor of peace, could not possibly enforce with precision. The justices quickly recognized that their task was to "construe" the Fourteenth Amendment "as it was understood at the time of its adoption,"[35] but they could not determine how it was understood when adopted because it had purposely been drafted so that different people

---

[34] 367 U.S. at 541–42.
[35] *Scott v. Sandford*, 60 U.S. (19 How.) 393, 426 (1857).

146   *William E. Nelson*

could understand it differently:[36] as the Republican state chair of Ohio explained to Chief Justice Salmon P. Chase in 1866, it was necessary in presenting the Fourteenth Amendment to the people "[i]n the Reserve Counties . . . [to] openly advocate impartial suffrage, while in other places . . . not only to repudiate it, but to oppose it."[37] As a result, although the justices were "in the condition of *seeking for truth*" in their efforts to construe the amendment,[38] they ultimately had to turn to the differing understandings of the people about the amendment's meaning.

The second reason why the Fourteenth Amendment can be read either as a flexible norm or as a permanent, inflexible guarantee is that its drafters and ratifiers wrote Section 1 so as to codify the higher law norms of the customary constitution. In my view, they did not codify specific, fixed norms. All that the framers did, on the basis of their understanding that states granted most higher law rights to their most favored citizens, was to insist that the states grant whatever rights they provided to any one citizen equally to all citizens.[39] On this view, states have power to modify the Fourteenth Amendment's meaning by altering the rights they provide to their most favored citizens.

Other scholars have theorized, however, that the language of privileges and immunities and due process directly incorporates specific norms into the constitution.[40] But even on this theory, there may be flexibility. The framers might have incorporated into the constitution not only specific higher law norms but also the customary constitution's understanding of the people's capacity over time to revise those norms. The speech that Thaddeus Stevens, a key drafter of the Fourteenth Amendment and its manager on the floor of the House of Representatives, made when he presented the amendment to the House supports this view. Although Stevens found the amendment an "imperfect . . . proposition," he argued that it was necessary

---

[36]See Nelson, *The Fourteenth Amendment*, pp. 142–44.

[37]B. R. Cowan to Salmon P. Chase, Oct. 12, 1866, in Salmon P. Chase Papers, Library of Congress, Washington, D.C.

[38]Joseph P. Bradley to Frederick T. Frelinghuysen, July 19, 1874, in Joseph P. Bradley Papers, New Jersey Historical Society, Newark, N.J. (emphasis in original).

[39]See Nelson, *The Fourteenth Amendment*, pp. 115–21.

[40]See Robert J. Kaczorowski, "The Supreme Court and Congress's Power to Enforce Constitutional Rights: An Overlooked Moral Anomaly," *Fordham Law Review* 73 (2004):153, 210–12, 217–30; Robert J. Kaczorowski, "Congress's Power to Enforce Fourteenth Amendment Rights: Lessons from Federal Remedies the Framers Enacted," *Harvard Journal of Legislation* 42 (2005):187, 207–30, 265–80.

The End of Popular Constitutionalism 147

to "take what we can get now, and hope for better things in further legislation; in enabling acts or other provisions"[41] as the amendment's meaning developed over time. On the other hand, the framers might have codified in permanent form the specific higher law norms that existed in 1866; the frequently reiterated language about the Fourteenth Amendment's permanence that I noted earlier supports this interpretation.

Despite occasional references to a "living constitution" and a "living tradition," the Supreme Court and constitutional scholars since the New Deal nonetheless have largely understood the Fourteenth Amendment to have codified a permanent, unchangeable set of principles. Both the court and scholars have tended to look back to the Reconstruction era to determine the content of those principles. Think, for example, of the debates about the Fourteenth Amendment's incorporation of the Bill of Rights[42] or about Congress's power under Section 5 to broaden the amendment's meaning.[43] Even in *Brown v. Board of Education*, the court began its analysis by directing counsel to inquire into original intent.[44] The customary constitution and the power of the people to give it meaning are, in large part, dead.

Paradoxically, a concern about the constitution's democratic pedigree is one reason for popular constitutionalism's demise. Chief Justice Taney in the *Dred Scott* case expressed this concern as well as anyone ever has. The constitution itself, he noted, prescribes how the people may amend it; for the court to usurp the power to change it would be "altogether inadmissible" for a "tribunal" of appointed, lifetime judges, who have power only "to interpret it."[45] But there is also another, deeper reason for popular constitutionalism's demise. If, as footnote 4 of *United States v. Carolene Products Co.* maintains, the main duty of the Supreme Court is to protect discrete and insular minorities,[46] it cannot do so by administering a constitution that the people have continuing power to revise. A customary constitution, subject to change at the will of some significant majority, sometimes will enable that majority to trample on the rights of politically powerless minorities.

---

[41] *Congressional Globe,* June 13, 1866, 39th Cong., 1st sess., p. 3148.

[42] Compare *Adamson v. California*, 332 U.S. 46, 68 (1947) (dissenting opinion of Justice Black) with Charles Fairman, "Does the Fourteenth Amendment Incorporate the Bill of Rights: The Original Understanding," *Stanford Law Review* 2 (1949):5.

[43] See *Oregon v. Mitchell*, 400 U.S. 112 (1970).

[44] See *Brown v. Board of Education*, 345 U.S. 972 (1953).

[45] *Scott v. Sandford*, 60 U.S. (19 How.) 393, 426 (1857).

[46] See *United States v. Carolene Products Co.*, 304 U.S. 144, 152 n.4 (1938).

One need only remember the internment of Japanese Americans during World War II or the long history of Jim Crow in the post–Civil War South. Minorities need the protection of robust, fixed principles that majorities cannot modify. Although a court charged with enforcing such principles may not always do so effectively, the existence of a constitution composed of fixed principles at least gives the court a chance.

So let me say this in conclusion. One way to think of a constitution—what we now see as the classic British way—is as a body of custom that people governed by the constitution can change over time. Alternatively, a constitution can be understood as a written guarantor of fixed rights. Americans today and often in the past have confusingly thought of their constitution as both. But the Civil War and the Reconstruction amendments brought a major shift in emphasis—from emphasis on a flexible constitution interpreted by the people to emphasis on a fixed guarantor of rights administered by forensic experts in the chambers of the Supreme Court.

Clay Risen

The Civil War at 100, the Civil War at 150

Commemoration, Identity, and the Changing Shape
of National Memory

IN 1961, THE poet and novelist Robert Penn Warren wrote, "The Civil War is, for the American imagination, the great single event of our history. Without too much wrenching, it may, in fact, be said to be American history." Even then, a century after Fort Sumter, he believed that the Civil War remained "our only 'felt' history—history that lived in the national imagination."[1]

When Warren wrote those words in his short, brilliant book *The Legacy of the Civil War*, the nation was just beginning to commemorate the conflict's centennial. It was a major undertaking: a presidentially appointed, blue-ribbon national panel, led by Ulysses S. Grant's grandson, was convened to coordinate scores of celebrations—and almost every state had its own separate commission. National parks were spruced up to accommodate hundreds of thousands of visitors. Stamps were issued. Coins were struck.

What a difference fifty years can make. Contrast those commemorative celebrations with the sesquicentennial that drew to a close in 2015. Again, stamps were issued. Coins were struck. But the recession of 2009 choked off incipient plans for a national commission, and no one seemed particularly bothered to protest. Few national events took place. And while crowds still visited battlefields, the numbers were smaller, and the commemorations

---

[1] Robert Penn Warren, *The Legacy of the Civil War* (1961; reprint ed., Lincoln, Neb., 1998), pp. 3–4.

149

150 *Clay Risen*

lower in key. If the centennial was a national event, the sesquicentennial, for many Americans, was more of a novelty, and a momentary one at that.

Maybe this is just the difference between a centennial and a sesquicentennial. It is not as if we as a country have decided that the Civil War did not matter. The Civil War still has great meaning as history—books about Lincoln, Grant, Stonewall Jackson, and other luminaries are guaranteed best sellers. But is the war any longer the "felt" history that Warren could so confidently assert it to be? And if not, what relevance does the Civil War have today?

First, let us examine why, besides the nice roundness of the number one hundred, the centennial was such a big deal in America—and what Warren meant by "felt" history.

For one thing, the Civil War was still very much present in American society. Albert Woolson, the last surviving verifiable Civil War veteran, had died just a few years earlier, in 1956. The country was still dotted with war widows, who in their youth had married aged veterans. And many Americans, Robert Penn Warren among them, had fond memories of growing up on the knee of a grandfather or great uncle who had fought in the war. Warren's grandfather, Gabriel Penn Warren, was a Confederate veteran who served with Nathan Bedford Forrest's cavalry. "He loved to relive the war with me," he told an interviewer. "We'd lay it all out on the ground using stones and rifle shells."[2]

The war was everywhere around him, from as far back as he could remember. In a 1961 interview, Warren said, "It was very much alive, not as an issue, but as a reality of life. It wasn't a matter of argument; it touched everyone's life. In this very static society, everyone you knew over a certain age had been in it . . . and it was just a part of the emotional furniture of life."[3]

Moreover, in 1961, unknowingly on the eve of Vietnam, the Civil War fit within a narrative of American wars as good wars. Commemorating the centennial as a fight for Union—which is how it was overwhelmingly celebrated—allowed Americans of the early 1960s to link their own sacrifices during World War II and Korea to this grand narrative of the national

---

[2] Peter Still, "An Interview with Robert Penn Warren," in Gloria L. Cronin and Ben Siegel, eds., *Conversations with Robert Penn Warren* (Jackson, Miss., 2005), p. 112.

[3] Interview with L. G. Bridson, 1961, cited in David W. Blight, *American Oracle: The Civil War in the Civil Rights Era* (Cambridge, Mass., 2011), p. 34.

The Civil War at 100, the Civil War at 150   151

martial experience. Men who marched as veterans of the twentieth-century wars could recall when, as boys, they watched much older men march as veterans of the Civil War.

But there was also a nervous tension about the centennial. As the historian Robert J. Cook describes in his book *Troubled Commemoration: The American Civil War Centennial*, President Dwight D. Eisenhower created the presidential commission in 1957, the same year that he sent federal troops into Little Rock, Arkansas, to enforce the Supreme Court's *Brown* decision.[4] Race relations—imbalanced yet largely static for nearly one hundred years—were being questioned. The meaning of the war as a fight for Union, as a war after which the white people on both sides reconciled, was beginning to be challenged—by a recalcitrant Jim Crow South as much as by civil rights activists.

It was all the more important, then, that the commission, under the president's direction, dramatize a single, overarching theme for its commemoration—namely, unionism and postwar reconciliation. The difficult, unanswered questions raised by the war—the meaning of freedom, the debts of white America for black enslavement, the country's acceptance of Jim Crow racism despite emancipation—were ignored. But they were ignored in part because they were ever more pressing; in 1961, the same year that the centennial began, the sit-in movement erupted in North Carolina. Four years earlier, Senator Lyndon B. Johnson had pushed through the first modern civil rights act, and now he was vice president. Change was coming, and the future was uncertain; but an embrace of the past, as a way of holding off that future, was still very much viable. For a moment, whites on both sides of the North-South divide could look back to the war as both a cautionary tale and a reminder that, in the end, they were all Americans, and leave aside the issue of where, if at all, black Americans fit into that equation.

And, of course, this was not a hard task. Anglo-Saxon, Protestant whites still dominated America, not just in the hegemonic sense but demographically. The United States was over 85 percent white. And even after the waves of migration at the turn of the past century, most American whites could reach back, not too far in their past, to find relatives who had fought in, or

---

[4]Peter J. Cook, *Troubled Commemoration: The American Civil War Centennial, 1961–1965* (Baton Rouge, La., 2007), p. 56.

at least lived through, the Civil War. (It goes without saying that the people leading the conversation about the war were all men.)

In short, the high profile of the centennial was achieved both because it had a strong base of support in a relatively unified white culture and because it responded to an unease within that culture about the very history it celebrated. It was "felt" history, at least for the moment.

Is it still "felt" history? Things are, obviously, very different today. First of all, there is the cultural and demographic distance. It is only fifty years later, but a lot has happened in those fifty years. As a boy, Warren could look around him in his small hometown of Guthrie, Kentucky, and see men, many of them related to him, who had fought in the war or had fathers and grandfathers who had. He could travel just south of the town to see the site where Confederate troops from Tennessee had invaded the state in 1861.

And yet, of course, Warren did not stay in Guthrie, and today even those of us who can trace our families back to the war have almost completely lost that sense of rootedness that was so important to a "felt" sense of Civil War history. My father was born in Nashville, not far from the Kentucky town where his parents were born, and on back down the family tree to a Union soldier from nearby named Wiley Patrick, who died outside Atlanta. In contrast, I was born in upstate New York, grew up in Nashville, moved to Washington, D.C., for college, and now live in New York City, where my children were born.

We do not just move around, we marry around. Again, consider my parents and ancestors. My mother is from Louisville, and she can trace her own history back to an Indiana soldier who died in Louisiana. My father's parents grew up just a few miles apart, in Kentucky. But I married a Jewish girl from Maine whose great grandparents immigrated from the Pale of Settlement. The parents of my children's friends are Pakistani, Japanese, and Nigerian. My children may someday dive into the history of the Civil War, but it will not be because it is, to them, "felt" history.

More dramatically, the demographic makeup of the country has changed. My children live in a world where whites, once the majority of the population, will likely represent less than 50 percent by the time they can vote. Today there are 129 million more Americans than there were in 1961—about a 60 percent increase in fifty years. One landmark often forgotten in recollections of the tumultuous 1960s was the passage of the 1965 Immigration Act not long after the end of the centennial commemoration, which opened the doors to national populations that had long been barred from our shores. As a result, today there are tens of millions of native-born Americans whose families were not here for the centennial of the Civil War, let alone the Civil War itself.

Along with that numerical change has come a cultural change. We may still be a white-majority country, but we are a decidedly multicultural country. There were Hispanic Americans in 1961, and Asian Americans, but the notion of mainstream Latin American culture, or Asian American culture, was by and large unthinkable. Today we celebrate these cultures, and even as we incorporate them into that ever-simmering soup called American culture, we also respect their identities and uniqueness. As a result, young people today look back to 1961 with only slightly more familiarity than they do to 1861.

Then there is the really dramatic stuff. Little did Americans in 1961, at the beginning of the Civil War centennial, know what they were about to go through: a civil rights revolution, a racial revolution, an immigration revolution, a feminist revolution, a whole long list of cultural revolutions that would fundamentally alter the meaning of "America."

As a result, we can no longer speak of "a" meaning of the Civil War, let alone any sort of collective "felt" history, because it is getting harder and harder to talk about American history with any sort of sense of consensus about its meaning. There are histories, not one single history, and different people will look at different parts of those histories differently. And while enormous debates will rage over how we interpret them—witness the renewed fight over slavery reparations and the role of racism in American history—most Americans are comfortable with the idea that no one historical account can speak for everyone.

Even to the extent that we can speak of any collective American historical view, it is one that is substantially more jaundiced today than it was in 1961. It is skeptical of, if not hostile to, patriotism, national symbols, the military, and calls for collective sacrifice—values that connected 1861 and 1961 but not 2011. If Americans in 1961 could look back one hundred years and imagine a moral world that largely echoed their own, that is much harder to do today.

Ironically, none of this would matter, really, if the Civil War were settled history, the way the Revolutionary War is (mostly) settled history. It might at one point have seemed settled, but the meaning of the Civil War has

154 *Clay Risen*

changed completely since 1961. More than changed—it has fractured. The events of the 1960s, and every decade since, have raised unanswered questions about the meaning of freedom, the role of the state in securing that freedom, the guilt of a country founded on race-based enslavement, and the failed promises of the war and postwar Reconstruction.

Let me take this irony a bit further. It may seem, in our lack of commemoration and fanfare over the sesquicentennial, that we are a much less historically minded people today than we were in 1961. It is easy, and common, for pundits to lament declining awareness of our past—fewer people reading history books, fewer resources for historical preservation, shrinking academic history departments. And it is true that we do not have, as Warren put it, a sense that the Civil War "stands there larger than life, massively symbolic in its inexhaustible and sibylline significance."[5]

In fact, I would argue that we are more historically minded than our predecessors. For all its inexhaustible significance, the popular history of the war in 1961 was still largely built on myth. Today we shatter myths; we are professionals at tearing down idols. Warren writes in awe of Lee and Jackson and Robert Gould Shaw and Sam Davis. But we know better. We might not pay heed to history in the same way people did in 1961, but that is to a large extent because we are skeptical about what "history" means. We refuse to accept history as a single narrative, as a pantheon of heroes and villains. Instead, we see history as an unfinished puzzle, to be contemplated instead of celebrated.

We understand that the Civil War, or rather its echo, still rings. Warren was looking back to a period rapidly drawing to a close; others, at the same time, saw a new one just beginning. Speaking at the Lincoln Memorial on August 28, 1963, just two years after Warren wrote his book, Martin Luther King Jr. intoned: "Five score years ago, a great American, in whose symbolic shadow we stand today, signed the Emancipation Proclamation." And yet, he said, "One hundred years later, the Negro lives on a lonely island of poverty in the midst of a vast ocean of material prosperity." The meaning of the Civil War, he said, was not complete and had to be contested:

> In a sense we've come to our nation's capital to cash a check. When the architects of our republic wrote the magnificent words of the Constitution and

---

[5]Warren, *The Legacy of the Civil War*, p. 80.

the Declaration of Independence, they were signing a promissory note to which every American was to fall heir. This note was a promise that all men, yes, black men as well as white men, would be guaranteed the "unalienable Rights" of "Life, Liberty and the pursuit of Happiness." It is obvious today that America has defaulted on this promissory note, insofar as her citizens of color are concerned. Instead of honoring this sacred obligation, America has given the Negro people a bad check, a check which has come back marked "insufficient funds." But we refuse to believe that the bank of justice is bankrupt. We refuse to believe that there are insufficient funds in the great vaults of opportunity of this nation. And so, we've come to cash this check, a check that will give us upon demand the riches of freedom and the security of justice.[6]

Life for minorities in America is inarguably better than it was in 1963, and yet the line "a lonely island of poverty in the midst of a vast ocean of material prosperity" could well describe Baltimore in 2015 or Ferguson or Baton Rouge or any number of poor, black neighborhoods and cities around the country. And the notion that civil rights activists are striving to "cash a check"—to call into question the meaning of the Civil War and demand that the country recognize its legacy—is only more salient today.

Every time we, as a nation, are reminded of this fact, we are also reminded of how the war was not a glorious triumph or a meaningful sacrifice, but rather one halting, tragic step in a story that continues to be told. And so, to answer my question, the Civil War is no longer "felt" history, but it is still vital history. If it can no longer be celebrated or mythologized, if we no longer rush to see it commemorated with parades and commissions, that does not mean we do not appreciate its importance. But we are no longer sure what that importance is—indeed, we are no longer sure that we will ever fully know what the war meant. We will continue to be fascinated by it, but we will do so not with self-righteousness or nostalgia or certainty but with skepticism, humility, and patience.

---

[6]Martin Luther King Jr., "I Have a Dream," Address Delivered at the March on Washington for Jobs and Freedom, King Papers, The Martin Luther King Jr. Research and Education Institute, Stanford University, https://kinginstitute.stanford.edu/king -papers/documents/i-have-dream-address-delivered-march-washington-jobs-and -freedom.

Contributors

Jenny Bourne is department chair and the Raymond Plank Professor of Economics at Carleton College in Northfield, Minnesota. She previously held positions at St. Olaf College and the U.S. Treasury Department. She is the author of *The Bondsman's Burden: An Economic Analysis of the Common Law of Southern Slavery* (Cambridge University Press, 1998), and *In Essentials, Unity: An Economic History of the Grange Movement* (Ohio University Press, 2017). Her current research includes a study of the relationship of income to wealth for the very rich and an analysis of the progressivity of the U.S. tax code.

Carole Emberton is associate professor of history at the University at Buffalo. She is the author of *Beyond Redemption: Race, Violence, and the American South after the Civil War* (University of Chicago Press, 2013) and numerous articles, including essays for national publications such as the *New York Times* and the *Washington Post*. She is currently working on a book about the Federal Writers' Project Ex-Slave Narratives, which will be published by W. W. Norton.

Paul Finkelman is the president of Gratz College in greater Philadelphia. Before coming to Gratz, he was the John E. Murray Visiting Professor of Law at the University of Pittsburgh School of Law, and also held the Fulbright Chair in Human Rights and Social Justice at the University of Ottawa College of Law. He has been a senior fellow at the Program on Democracy, Citizenship, and Constitutionalism at the University of Pennsylvania and a scholar-in-residence at the National Constitution Center. In 2016 he held the Ariel F. Sallows Chair in Human Rights at the University of Saskatchewan College of Law. He is the author or editor of more than fifty books and two hundred scholarly articles.

Lorien Foote is the Patricia and Bookman Peters Professor of History and director of graduate studies in the History Department at Texas A&M University. She is the author of three books about the American Civil War, including *The Gentlemen and the Roughs: Manhood, Honor, and Violence in the Union Army* (NYU Press, 2010), which was an honorable mention for the 2011 Lincoln Prize, and *The Yankee Plague: Escaped Union Prisoners and the Collapse of the Confederacy* (University of North Carolina Press, 2016), which was a *Choice* Outstanding Academic

158   *Contributors*

Title. She is currently working on a book about civilized warfare and the practice of retaliation.

William E. Nelson is the Judge Edward Weinfeld Professor of Law at the New York University School of Law. Nelson has published two prize-winning books, eight other books, and numerous articles in leading law reviews and history journals. He is the author of *The Fourteenth Amendment: From Political Principle to Judicial Doctrine* (Harvard University Press, 1998) and the four-volume *The Common Law in Colonial America* (Oxford University Press, 2008–18). Nelson has focused in his upper-year curriculum on training future law teachers, especially in his seminar on legal scholarship.

Clay Risen is the deputy op-ed editor at the *New York Times*. In addition to writing on American history, he is a leading authority on the history, business, and diversity of U.S. spirits. His best seller, *American Whiskey, Bourbon and Rye: A Guide to the Nation's Favorite Spirit* (Sterling Epicure, 2013), is now in its sixth printing. His publications on American history include *A Nation on Fire: America in the Wake of the King Assassination* (Wiley, 2009), *The Bill of the Century: The Epic Battle for the Civil Rights Act* (Bloomsbury, 2014), and *The Crowded Hour: Teddy Roosevelt, the Rough Riders and the Dawn of the American Century* (forthcoming 2019).

Anne Sarah Rubin is professor of history and associate director of the Imaging Research Center at the University of Maryland, Baltimore County. The project also has a multimedia component, which can be found at http://www.shermansmarch.org. She is the coeditor of *The Perfect Scout: A Soldier's Memoir of the Great March to the Sea and the Campaign of the Carolinas* (University of Alabama Press, 2018) and the author of *Through the Heart of Dixie: Sherman's March in American Memory* (University of North Carolina Press, 2014). Her first book, *A Shattered Nation: The Rise and Fall of the Confederacy* (University of North Carolina Press, 2005), received the 2006 Avery O. Craven Award from the Organization of American Historians for the most original book on the Civil War era.

Peter Wallenstein is professor of history at Virginia Polytechnic Institute and State University, where he specializes in the history of the U.S. South, Virginia, civil rights, and higher education. He is the author or editor of many books, including *Cradle of America: A History of Virginia* (2nd ed. rev., University Press of Kansas, 2014), *Blue Laws and Black Codes: Conflict, Courts, and Change in Twentieth-Century Virginia* (University of Virginia Press, 2004), *Tell the Court I Love My Wife: Race, Marriage, and Law—An American History* (Palgrave Macmillan, 2002), and *From Slave South to New South: Public Policy in Nineteenth-Century Georgia* (University of North Carolina Press, 1987).

Index

abolitionists, 77, 140–41

Act of Settlement (1761), 136

Adams, John, 106, 108

African Americans: emancipation, 7; enfranchisement, 126; forced labor of, 95; hunger at end of Civil War, 11–23; illiteracy among, 94; interviews of in 1930s, 12; as landowners and income of, 44; in postwar South, 51; postwar status of, 105; reenslavement, postwar threat of, 100; Sherman's employment of, 64; suffrage, 112–13, 119; Union military, service and pay in, 1, 45, 89–90; violence directed at in postwar South, 96–101. *See also* Black Codes, Southern; Fifteenth Amendment; Fourteenth Amendment; Norfolk, Virginia, convention and manifesto of black Southerners (1865); Thirteenth Amendment

agriculture, postwar, 41

Alabama, black codes in, 93–94

Aldrich, Chauncey S., 32

American Gazetteer, 139

American Union Aid Commission, 14

Anderson, "Bloody Bill," 5

Andersonville Prison, 8, 24, 38

Andrews, Christopher C., 94

Appomattox, Virginia, surrender at, 104, 112

Arkansas, post–Civil War state constitution, 95

Army of Virginia, 58

Ashley, James, 86

Atlanta, Georgia, expulsion by Sherman of civilians from, 62

Bank of the United States, First, 140

Bank of the United States, Second, 140

Banner, James, 106

Barnard, R. W., 97

Bayne, Thomas, 111, 126, 129

Belgium, German occupation of in World War I compared to Sherman's March, 67, 68

Benton Barracks (St. Louis, Missouri), 32

Berger, Raoul, 77, 81, 84

Berwanger, Eugene, 76, 81

Bigelow, John A., 69–70

Bill of Rights, 147

Bingham, John A.: and Fourteenth Amendment, 101–2; and Joint Committee on Reconstruction, 76, 91; and race relations in Ohio, 84–89; and readmission of Tennessee, 96

Black Codes, Southern, 91, 92–96, 110, 131, 134

Blaine, James G., 109

Bond, James E., 122–24

Booth, Benjamin, 32–33

Boston Tea Party, 135

Bourne, Jenny, 8, 9

Boutwell, George S., 91

Brinkerhoff, Jacob, 86, 88

Brown v. Board of Education (1954), 74–75, 151

Buchanan, James, 82

Burden of Southern History, The (Woodward), 72

Bureau of Refugees, Freedmen, and Abandoned Lands. *See* Freedmen's Bureau

Burrell, Savilla, 11

Calhoun, James M., 62–63

Cameron, Simon, 83

Camp Ford, Texas, 26

Camp Parole, Annapolis, Maryland, 31, 32

Carnegie, Andrew, 43–44

Carr, Matthew, 55

Charleston, South Carolina, 46

Chase, Salmon P., 86, 88, 146

Christiana (Pennsylvania) incident, 78–80

Circular No. 11 (1865), 19

Civil Rights Act of 1866, 9–10, 91, 96, 105, 115, 119, 131, 134

Civil War: amendments, constitutional, 24; casualties in, 4–5; centennial and sesquicentennial commemorations of, 149–55; constitutional issues after, 143–48;

159

160 *Index*

Civil War (cont.)
cost of, human and financial, 4–7;
devastation after, 1, 6, 9; impact on
U.S. economy, 39–53; meaning of, 153.
See also African Americans: Sherman's
employment of; African Americans: Union
military, service and pay in; Andersonville
Prison; Appomattox, Virginia, surrender
at; Atlanta, Georgia, expulsion by
Sherman of civilians from; Camp Ford,
Texas; Camp Parole, Annapolis, Maryland;
Emancipation Proclamation; "felt history,"
Civil War as; Fifteenth Amendment;
Fort Fisher, North Carolina; Fort Pillow,
Tennessee; Fourteenth Amendment;
Freedmen's Bureau; Grand Army of the
Republic; guerrillas, Confederate; Hood,
John Bell; Hunter, David, Shenandoah
Valley Campaign; Jackson, Thomas J.
"Stonewall"; Lieber Code; prisoners of
war; prisons, Confederate; Richmond,
Virginia, devastation after Civil War;
Sherman, William T.: March to the Sea;
Wilmington, North Carolina, prisoner of
war exchange
Clapp, Dexter H., 99
Code for the Government of Armies, A (Lieber), 59
commemorations. *See* Civil War: centennial
and sesquicentennial commemorations of
Commerce Clause, 109
commodity money, 44
Congress, United States. *See* United States
Congress
Conkling, Roscoe, 118, 129
Constitution, English, 136–37
Constitutional Convention of 1787, 105, 106
constitutionalism, antislavery, 141
constitutionalism, customary, concept of, 137,
146
constitutionalism, popular, concept of, 135,
137, 141, 147
constitutionalism, secessionist, 141
Constitution of the United States.
See Commerce Clause; Constitutional
Convention of 1787; contract clause
(U.S. Constitution); Fifteenth Amendment;
Fourteenth Amendment; Fugitive Slave
Clause; originalism; slavery, and the
Constitution of the United States;
Thirteenth Amendment; Three-Fifths
Clause

constitutions, state, 1776–80, 138
Continental Congress, First, 108
Continental Congress, Second, 108
contract clause (U.S. Constitution), 139–40
Cook, Robert J., 151
Cooke, Jay, 44
Cooper v. Aaron (1958), 135–36
currency. *See* commodity money; fiat money
Curtis, George William, 125
Custer, George Armstrong, 100

Dalton, Georgia, 5, 8, 26
Davis, Sam, 154
Declaration of Independence (1776), 138,
141
Declaration of Rights (1689), 136
De Forest, John W., 20, 21
demographic change, in post-Civil War
United States, 152–53
Dependent Pension Act (1890), 37–38
Dickinson, John, 138
Douglass, Frederick, 78
Dred Scott v. Sandford (1857), 142, 143, 147
Dunning, William A., 116
Dunning historians, 132

economy, post-Civil War, 39–53
Eisenhower, Dwight D., 151
elections, congressional (1866), 125
Electoral College, 127–28
Emancipation Proclamation, 7, 90
Emberton, Carole, 3

farmers, economic problems of post-Civil
War, 46–48
Federal Writers Project, 12
Fellman, Michael, 65
"felt history," Civil War as, 149, 151, 152,
155
Fessenden, William Pitt, 116, 118
fiat money, 44–45
Field Service in War (Lippitt), 60–61
Fifteenth Amendment, 10, 12, 74, 126
Fillmore, Millard, 78
Fincher, Stephen, 21
Finkelman, Paul, 1
First Iowa Cavalry, 26
Fisk, Clinton, 97
Fletcher v. Peck (1810), 139
Florida, post-Civil War state constitution, 95
Foner, Eric, 128–29

Index 161

Foote, Lorien, 3, 5, 7, 8
Ford, Ford Madox, 70–71
Foreign Policy, 73
Formans v. Tamm (1853), 82
Forno, Henry, 29
Forrest, Nathan Bedford, 150
Fort Fisher, North Carolina, 27
Fort Pillow, Tennessee, 5
Forty-Fourth United States Colored
    Troops, 26
Forty-Seventh Congress, 37
Founding Fathers, 136, 141
Fourteenth Amendment, 1, 10, 12; Joint
    Committee on Reconstruction and,
    74–102; popular constitutionalism and,
    144–48; ratification of, 120, 125, 126;
    Section 1, 84, 105, 145–46; Section 2,
    103–34; Section 3, 131; Section 4, 119;
    Section 5, 119, 147; white Southerners
    and, 122–24
Freedmen's Bureau, 93, 100, 111; criticisms of,
    21; relief efforts of, 13–15, 17–21
Freedmen's Bureau Bill (1866), 16, 115, 118,
    119, 134
Freehling, William W., 109
Free Soilers, in Ohio, 89
Frontier against Slavery, The (Berwanger), 76
Fugitive Slave Clause, 81
Fugitive Slave Law, Federal, 81
Fugitive Slave Law of 1850, 88
fugitive slaves, law regulating in Ohio, 86

General Orders No. 100, 59
Geneva Convention, 58
Georgia: kidnapping and reenslavement
    of African Americans post-Civil War,
    100–101; state constitution post-Civil
    War, 96
Gettysburg Address, 10
Gilded Age, 44
Goldberg, Chad, 20
Goldsboro, North Carolina, 28, 30
Google Alert, 73
Grand Army of the Republic, 34
Granger movement, 46
Grant, Ulysses S., 45, 71, 140, 150
"Great Tablecloth, The" (Neruda), 22–23
Grimsley, Mark, 58
guerrillas, Confederate, 59. *See also* Anderson,
    "Bloody Bill"; James, Frank; James, Jesse;
    Younger brothers

Guntharpe, Violet, 12, 13, 22
Guthrie, Kentucky, 152

Hague Convention, 58
Halleck, Henry, 58
Ham, Cindy, 22
Hamilton, Alexander, 139
Hamlin, Hannibal, 121–22
Hampton, Wade, 65, 71
Harlan, John Marshall II, 144
Harper, Robert Goodloe, 139
Harper's Weekly, 125
Harris, William C., 128, 129
Hartford Convention, 106, 107–8, 110, 119
Hatch, Edward, 97
Henderson, Yendell, 69, 69
Henry County, Georgia, 55
Hess, Michael, 71
Hitchcock, Henry, 61
Hoke, Robert F., 27
Homestead Act, 42
Hood, John Bell, 62–63
Hookworm, 51
Hotchkiss, John B., 38
House of Representatives. *See* United States
    House of Representatives
Howard, Charles H., 100
Howard, Oliver Otis, 17, 19
hunger, and starvation in post-Civil War, 3–4,
    11–23
Hunter, David, Shenandoah Valley Campaign
    (1864), 67

immigrants, post-Civil War, 51
immigration, 42
Immigration Act of 1965, 152–53
internment, of Japanese Americans in World
    War II, 148
Iowa City, Iowa, 33
Iraq War, compared to Sherman's March, 73

Jackson, Andrew, 51
Jackson, Thomas J. "Stonewall", 71, 150, 154
Jacksonian democracy, 81
James, Frank, 5
James, Jesse, 5
James, Joseph B., 122
Japanese Americans, internment of in World
    War II, 148
Jefferson, Thomas, 106
Jim Crow laws, 148, 151

162 Index

Johnson, Andrew, 104; and Reconstruction, 110; veto of Civil Rights Act of 1866, 131, 134; veto of Freedmen's Bureau Bill (1866), 16, 118, 121, 134
Johnson, Lyndon, 151
Johnson, William, 140
Joint Committee on Reconstruction, 74–102; creation of, 91; and Fourteenth Amendment, 91–92; report of, 91–92
Jones, Mary Cadwallader, 68
Jordan, Brian Matthew, 37
Juneteenth, 26

Kansas-Nebraska Act, 109
Keifer, Joseph Warren, 37
Kelly, William D., 83
Kendrick, Benjamin B., 116, 132
Key West, Florida, 38
Kinder, Donald, 22
King, Martin Luther Jr., 154–55
Korean Conflict, 150

LaBaume, Felix, 36
Larrabee, Silas (pseud.), 66
laws of war. See war, laws of
Lee, Robert E., 5, 71, 154
Legacy of the Civil War, The (Warren), 149
Levine, Howard, 71
Lewis, Ellis, 82–83
Lieber, Francis, and laws of war, 58–60
Lieber Code, 59–60, 61
Liège, Belgium, 71
Lincoln (motion picture), 103
Lincoln, Abraham: biographers of, 128–30; books about, 150; Gettysburg Address, 10; and Preliminary Emancipation Proclamation, 58; second inaugural address, 22; second inauguration, 104
Lincoln and Reconstruction (Rodrigue), 129
Lincoln Memorial, 154
Lippitt, Francis J., 60–61
Little Rock, Arkansas, 151
Litwack, Leon, 76, 81
Livingston, Philip, 138
Lodge, Henry Cabot, 66
lost-cause partisans, 9
Louisiana Purchase, 106
Lowery, Grosvenor, 141

Mach, Edmund von, 70
Madison, James, 107

Magna Carta, 136
manufacturing, post-Civil War, 41
Marshall, John, 102, 139, 140, 142
McCarthy, Mary, 71
McCulloch v. Maryland (1819), 102, 140, 142
Medal of Honor, Congressional, 99
Memphis, Tennessee, 24, 131
military necessity, 59, 60
Mississippi, black codes in, 93, 94–95, 111
Mississippi Civil Rights Act of 1865, 94
Mississippi River, 24
Missouri Crisis (1819–20), 106, 109
Mitchell, Margaret, 4
modern war, and Sherman's March, 66–73. See also total war
Monroe Doctrine, 67
Morgan, Margaret, 81
Morrill, Justin S., 91
Morse, Jedidiah, 139

Napoleon's Russian Campaign, 61
National Ex-Prisoners of War Association, 36
national parks, 149
"Negro President": Jefferson and the Slave Power (Wills), 106
Nelson, Knute, 70
Nelson, William E., 1, 122
Neruda, Pablo, 22–23
New Deal, 147
New Orleans, Louisiana, 31
New York Times, 66, 67, 68, 69
Norfolk, Virginia, convention and manifesto of black Southerners (1865), 111–12, 118
North Carolina, post-Civil War violence against African Americans, 99
Northeast Cape Fear River, 29, 30, 34

Ohio, personal liberty laws (1839), 87
Ohio Association of Union Ex-Prisoners of War, 37
originalism, interpretation of United States Constitution, 144
Otis, James Jr., 137

Parliament, 135, 136
patent activity, post-Civil War, 42, 50–51
Patrick, Wiley, 152
Pease, Jane, 77
Pease, William, 77
Pennsylvania, race relations and law pre-Civil War, 78–83

Index 163

Pennsylvania Constitutional Convention (1837), 78
Pennsylvania Personal Liberty Law (1826), 81
Pennsylvania Supreme Court, 82
Pension Bureau, 35
pensions. *See* prisoners of war: pensions for
Philippine Insurrection, United States military campaign compared to Sherman's March, 66
Poe v. Ullman (1961), 144
poll tax, 95
Pope, John, 58
Powell, Jefferson, 137
Prigg, Edward, 81
Prigg v. Pennsylvania (1842), 81, 82, 142, 14
prisoners of war: Confederate, at end of Civil War, 3; exchanges of, 24–26, 27–31; pensions for, 35–38; as political issue, 34; processing and return home, 32–34; recovery and trauma, 35; Union, at end of Civil War, 3, 7–8, 24–38
prisons, Confederate, 24–26. *See also* Andersonville prison
Putnam, George Haven, 68

race, and law in pre-Civil War North, 76–78
race relations, law of, 75, 97–100, 131
racial violence, in post-Civil War South, 75
Radical Reconstruction. *See* Reconstruction: Congressional
railroads, post-Civil War growth, 42, 46
recession of 2009, 149
Reconstruction: amendments, 143; Congressional, 124–27; failed promises of, 154; politics of, historicizing the, 103–34; Southern context of, 89–101. *See also* Bingham, John A.; Civil Rights Act of 1866; Dunning, William A.; Fifteenth Amendment; Fourteenth Amendment; Johnson, Andrew; Joint Committee on Reconstruction; *Lincoln and Reconstruction* (Rodrigue); Norfolk, Virginia, convention and manifesto of black Southerners (1865); Sherman, John; Sherman, William T.; Stevens, Thaddeus
Reconstruction: America's Unfinished Revolution, 1863–1877 (Foner), 128–29
Reconstruction, Political and Economic, 1865–1877 (Dunning), 116
Redeemer governments, 52
Reid, John Phillip, 136

Repository (Franklin County, Pennsylvania), 125
Republican Party: antislavery constitutionalism, 141; congressional leaders, 78; 1868 election campaigns, 34; in Ohio, 86, 89
Reston, James Jr., 55, 72
Restoration, of Southern states to Union, 104. *See also* Reconstruction
Richmond, Virginia, devastation after Civil War, 1
Ricks, Thomas, 73
Risen, Clay, 4, 10
robber barons, 44
Robinson, James S., 37
Rockefeller, John D., 44
Rodrigue, John C., 129
Rosengarten, Theodore, 71
Rubin, Anne Sarah, 1

Saxton, Rufus, 99–100
Schofield, John M., 27
Schooner, John, 38
Schurz, Carl, 90
Scott, Henry, 26, 27
Scott v. Sandford. See *Dred Scott v. Sandford* (1857)
sectionalism, and Fourteenth Amendment, 135–48
Senate Committee on Propaganda (1919), 70
Seventh Connecticut, 30
Shaw, Robert Gould, 154
Sheridan, Phillip, 71
Sherman, John: and Reconstruction, 112–13, 121, 127, 129; and resumption of commodity money, 45
Sherman, Texas, 26
Sherman, William T.: and laws of war, 58–66; March to the Sea, 1, 4, 6, 54–73; popular opinions about, 54–55; and Reconstruction, 112–13, 118–19, 121; supplies diverted from for exchanged prisoners of war, 31; as terrorist, 65–66; Winnsboro, South Carolina, surrender of, 11. *See also* Belgium, German occupation of in World War I compared to Sherman's March; Iraq War, compared to Sherman's March; Philippine Insurrection, United States military campaign compared to Sherman's March; Vietnam War, compared to Sherman's March; World War I, compared to Sherman's March

164 *Index*

"Sherman as a Counterinsurgent" (Ricks), 73
Sherman's Ghosts: Soldiers, Civilians, and the American Way of Life (Carr), 55
Sherman's Laws, 61–66
Sherman's March and Vietnam (Reston), 72
Sherman's March to the Sea. *See* Sherman, William T.: March to the Sea
slavery, and Constitution of the United States, 141–43
slave trade, interstate, 109
Sloane, William M., 67
Smith, George B., 98
Smith, Jacob H., 66
Soule, Charles, 17
South: conditions in at end of Civil War, 3, 6–7; economy post–Civil War, 48–50
South Carolina, post–Civil War violence against African Americans in, 99–100
Southern Compromise Agreement, 123
Southern racial violence against African Americans in 1866, 131
Southern state constitutions (1865–66), 92–96
Southern state legislatures post–Civil War, 90
Southern whites: condemnation of Reconstruction, 16; hunger post–Civil War, 15; violence against African Americans post–Civil War, 99–100, 131
Special Field Orders No. 67, 62
Special Field Orders No. 120, 64
Spencer, Barnett, 12
Spielberg, Steven, 103
Spooner, Lysander, 140–41
Squires, Grant, 70
Stevens, Thaddeus: and Fourteenth Amendment, 76, 101–2, 146–47; and Joint Committee on Reconstruction, 91, 115; and race relation in Pennsylvania, 78–83
Story, Joseph, 142
Sultana (steamship) explosion, 24
Sumner, Charles, 96
Sunshine (steamship), 32
Supplemental Nutrition Assistance Program (SNAP), 21
Supreme Court of the United States, 136. See also *Brown v. Board of Education* (1954); *Cooper v. Aaron* (1958); *Dred Scott v. Sandford* (1857); *Fletcher v. Peck* (1810); Harlan, John Marshall II; Marshall, John; *McCulloch v. Maryland* (1819); *Poe v. Ullman* (1961); *Prigg v. Pennsylvania* (1842); Story, Joseph; Taney,

Roger B.; *United States v. Carolene Products Co.* (1938)

Taney, Roger B., 142, 147
Tennessee: and ratification of Fourteenth Amendment, 122; violence against African Americans post–Civil War, 97–98
Terry, Alfred H., 31
Texas: black codes in, 94; violence against African Americans post–Civil War, 100
Third New Hampshire, 30
Thirteenth Amendment, 7, 74, 90, 95, 103, 104
Thirty-Eighth Congress, 104
Thirty-Ninth Congress, 74, 104
Thirty-Seventh Congress, 42
Three-Fifths Clause: end of, 131–34; history of (1787–1861), 105–110; and Norfolk convention, 111–12; postemancipation, 109–10
Three-Fifths Compromise, 105
total war, Sherman, and concept of, 55. *See also* war, laws of
To the Hartford Convention (Banner), 106
transcontinental railroad, 42
transportation costs, post–Civil War, 42
Trevelyan, G. M., 68
Troubled Commemoration: The American Civil War Centennial (Cooke), 151
Turner, John W., 98, 112

underground railroad, 53
Underwood, John C., 98–99
Unionists, 143
Unionists, white Southern, 92, 93
Union Party, 121
United States Congress. *See* Civil Rights Act of 1866; Dependent Pension Act (1890); elections, congressional (1866); Fifteenth Amendment; Forty-Seventh Congress; Freedmen's Bureau Bill (1866); Homestead Act; Immigration Act of 1965; Joint Committee on Reconstruction; Kansas-Nebraska Act; Reconstruction: Congressional; Senate Committee on Propaganda (1919); Supplemental Nutrition Assistance Program (SNAP); Thirty-Eighth Congress; Thirty-Ninth Congress; Thirty-Seventh Congress; United States House of Representatives
United States Constitution. *See* Constitution of the United States

United States House of Representatives: investigation of treatment of prisoners of war, 34; representation in, issue of, 105. *See also* Fourteenth Amendment, Section 2; Three-Fifths Clause

United States Sanitary Commission, 31

United States v. Carolene Products Co. (1938), 147

Urban Dictionary (website), 54

Us against Them: Ethnocentric Foundations of American Opinion (Kinder and Hamm), 22

Van Cleve, George William, 106

Vicksburg, Mississippi, 24

Vietnam War, compared to Sherman's March, 71–73, 150

Virginia, violence against African Americans post-Civil War, 98–99

wages, post-Civil War, 49–50

Wallenstein, Peter, 1

war, laws of, 55, 58–61. See also *Field Service in War* (Lippitt); Lieber, Francis; Lieber Code; Lippitt, Francis J.; military necessity; modern war; Sherman, William T.; Sherman's Laws; total war

War of 1812, 106

War of Independence, 135

Warren, Gabriel Penn, 150

Warren, Robert Penn, 149–50, 154

wealth, personal, post-Civil War, 43–44

Webster, Daniel, 78

Webster, Noah, 138–39

Welch, Robert, 66

Westmoreland, William, 72

westward migration, post-Civil War, 42

Wills, Garry, 106

Wilmington, North Carolina, prisoner of war exchange, 24, 27–31

Wirz, Henry, 8–9

Woodward, C. Vann, 72

Woolson, Albert, 150

World War I, compared to Sherman's March, 4, 71–73

World War II, 148, 150

Younger brothers, 5